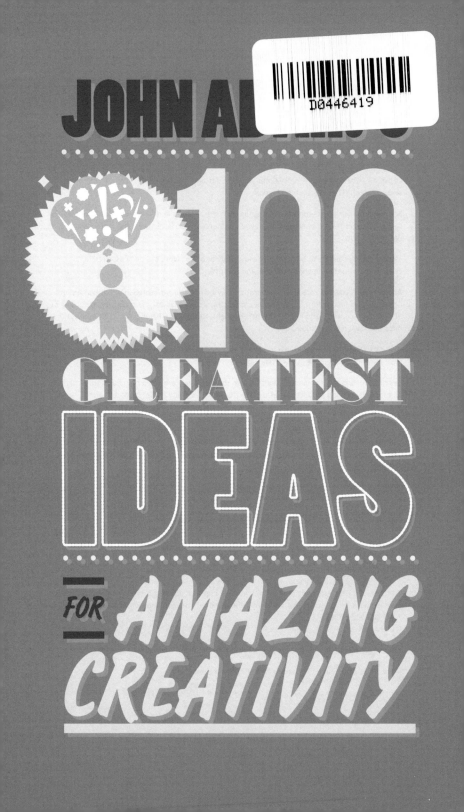

This edition first published 2011
© 2011 John Adair

Registered office
Capstone Publishing Ltd. (A Wiley Company), The Atrium, Southern Gate, Chichester,
West Sussex, PO19 8SQ, United Kingdom

For details of our global editorial offices, for customer services and for information about how
to apply for permission to reuse the copyright material in this book please see our website at
www.wiley.com.

The right of the author to be identified as the author of this work has been asserted in
accordance with the Copyright, Designs and Patents Act 1988.

All rights reserved. No part of this publication may be reproduced, stored in a retrieval system,
or transmitted, in any form or by any means, electronic, mechanical, photocopying, recording or
otherwise, except as permitted by the UK Copyright, Designs and Patents Act 1988, without the
prior permission of the publisher.

Wiley also publishes its books in a variety of electronic formats. Some content that appears in
print may not be available in electronic books.

Designations used by companies to distinguish their products are often claimed as trademarks.
All brand names and product names used in this book are trade names, service marks,
trademarks or registered trademarks of their respective owners. The publisher is not associated
with any product or vendor mentioned in this book. This publication is designed to provide
accurate and authoritative information in regard to the subject matter covered. It is sold on the
understanding that the publisher is not engaged in rendering professional services. If
professional advice or other expert assistance is required, the services of a competent
professional should be sought.

Library of Congress Cataloguing-in-Publication Data

Adair, John, 1934–
   John Adair's greatest ideas for amazing creativity/John Adair.
      p.cm.
Includes index.
9780857081766 (paperback), ISBN 9780857082268 (ebk),
ISBN 9780857082275 (ebk), ISBN 9780857082282 (ebk)
   1. Creative ability in business.   2. Creative thinking.   3. Success in business.
   I. Title.   II. Title: John Adair's Hundred greatest ideas for amazing creativity.   III. Title: 100
greatest ideas for amazing creativity.   IV. Title: Hundred greatest ideas for amazing creativity.
   HD53. A318 2011
   658.4′094–dc23

A catalogue record for this book is available from the British Library.

Set in 10/13 pt Calibri by Toppan Best-set Premedia Limited

Printed and bound in Great Britain by TJ International Ltd. Padstow, Cornwall.

Author's Note

Effective business people have fine-tuned leadership and management ability backed up by exceptional decision-making, communication and creative skills and the know-how to implement it all successfully. These six areas are the basis of the 100 Greatest series.

None of these skills stands alone, all are interconnected, and for that reason I've revisited key ideas across the series. If you read more than one book, as I hope you will, you'll meet key ideas more than once. These are the framework on which the series hangs and the repetition will help you become a master of modern business.

Likewise, if you only read one book, the inclusion of key ideas from across the series means that you'll benefit from seeing your chosen subject within the wider context of leadership and management excellence.

Good luck on your journey to becoming an effective manager within your organization.

John Adair

Contents

100 Greatest Ideas . . . in an instant!

Whether you're a first time manager or an experienced leader, running a small team or an entire organization, straightforward, practical advice is hard to find.

John Adair's 100 Greatest Ideas . . . are the building blocks for an amazing career, putting essential business skills and must-have thinking at your fingertips.

The ideas are short, punchy and clustered around themes, so you'll find answers to all your questions quickly and easily. Everything you need to be simply brilliant is here, and it's yours in an instant.

Look out for these at-a-glance features:

Personal Mantra –
Powerful statements as a source for inspiration

Ask Yourself –
Questions to get you thinking most about the information

Remind Yourself –
Key points to help you reflect on the Ideas

Checklist –

A list of questions to help you put the Ideas into practice

100 Greatest Ideas . . . 6 Great Books

John Adair's 100 Greatest Ideas for Effective Leadership

John Adair's 100 Greatest Ideas for Personal Success

John Adair's 100 Greatest Ideas for Brilliant Communication

John Adair's 100 Greatest Ideas for Smart Decision Making

John Adair's 100 Greatest Ideas for Amazing Creativity

John Adair's 100 Greatest Ideas for Being a Brilliant Manager

Preface

As a leader – whatever your field – you are the one responsible for finding the right ideas. You may not be the author of the ideas yourself. But you do need resourcefulness, a proper sense of timing for when conditions are ripe for a given idea and also, of course, judgement and the capability to select the best ideas from those presented to you. Ideas are a leader's business.

The ideas I am talking about may relate to any aspect of your team's or organization's common endeavour, ranging from incremental improvements in its normal flow of activities to really significant innovations and major changes. For creativity embraces not only having the right idea, but also giving it objective existence.

Your own creative talent in the mental realm may not be called for, but you certainly need to understand creativity in others, and how to manage it effectively.

Part One begins with a brief introduction – a welcoming one, I hope – to the concepts of creativity and innovation. Then I offer you a model of how your mind works, especially in its more creative dimensions.

Part Two both identifies your creative thinking skills and gives you an opportunity to develop them by some simple practices. There is no one who cannot increase their capacity to generate ideas if they are willing to study and practise.

Part Three explores more fully the ways in which inventors, discoverers and artists find their ideas – or their ideas find them. It isn't that I expect you to become one of them. It's more that by studying how great imaginative or creative minds work, you can pick up some useful tips for making the best of your own imagination.

Part Four lets you in on a secret. For one reason or another you may find it hard to have ideas. But others don't seem to have that problem. So why not capitalize on their ideas? The creative team leader – the hero of Part Four – does just that. Here's an opportunity for you to acquire their skills.

Part Five argues that your whole organization should become creative and innovative. Creative thinking – new ideas great and small – is everyone's business, not just the manager's. As John Buchan said: 'The task of leadership is not to put greatness into people but to elicit it, for the greatness is there already.' This is the challenge for today's leaders.

This organizational capacity to generate ideas, harvest the best and – through effective teamwork – make them effective and real doesn't happen by chance. It calls for strategic leadership of the highest order. Are you ready for it?

John Adair

PART ONE

Find Your Own Creative Mind

Man is pre-eminently a creative animal, predestined to strive consciously for an object and to engage in building – that is, incessantly and eternally to make new roads, wherever they may lead.

Fyodor Dostoevski, Russian novelist

Creativity, creative thinking and even innovation are terms used so widely and so often that they are now in danger of losing their meaning altogether.

The first cluster of Ideas in Part One not only restores their meanings but also serves – I hope – as a personal invitation for you to consider yourself a creative and innovative individual. It's your self-perception that matters.

That journey to the more creative *you* begins by exploring briefly the wonder of the human mind, that most extraordinary of all creations.

Part One covers how your mind works: its three principal functions, the role of your unconscious or depth mind and how feeling or emotion is always in the picture.

Dostoevski's words quoted above ring true. The human mind *is* made for creativity and innovation. In that fact lies the ultimate salvation of the human race on earth. And it means that there is no reason you or I will ever run out of ideas.

Six Greatest Ideas for Creativity and Innovation

Idea 1: Four ways of causing something new to exist

To create is always to do something new.

Martin Luther, German theologian who
inspired the Protestant Reformation

'It seems almost impossible, Mr Ford,' a visitor once told the industrialist, 'that a man, starting 25 years ago with practically nothing, could accomplish all this.'

'You say that I started with practically nothing,' Henry Ford replied, 'but that's hardly correct. Every man starts with all there is. Everything is here – the essence and substance of all there is.'

Henry Ford was philosophically right. The potential materials – the elements, constituents or substances of which something can be made or composed – are indeed all here in our universe. We humans cannot make something out of nothing.

If you narrowly define creativity as 'to bring a thing into existence without any previous material at all to work on', as Thomas Aquinas did, then clearly it is, as it has been said, 'only God who creates – Man rearranges'. Our human creativity is similar but not equivalent to the powers or effects ascribed traditionally to the Supreme Being. It is against that background that we can explore four basic forms of human activity that involve creative thinking:

1   *Making* – Our most general term for causing something to come into being, but it usually implies the physical or figurative handling of materials. Ford was a maker of cars, or, more precisely, a manufacturer, one who makes something repeatedly by a fixed process and usually by machinery.

2 *Inventing* – Means fabricating something useful, usually as a result of ingenious thinking or experiment.

3 *Discovery* – Presupposes the pre-existence of something and implies finding rather than making.

4 *Creating* – Seldom suggests either literal or figurative use or handling of materials. Its leading implication is bringing into existence what the mind conceives and the will – as the mind's instrument – carries out. Creating what is brought into existence, the finished product, is very different from the materials used in its making. That is why believing people have called God the Creator rather than the Maker.

Creative thinking is about having new ideas, but creativity – the business of creation – is a much wider term. *It is the entire process whereby things that did not exist before are conceived, given form and brought into being.*

Remember the fundamental point that as human beings we never create from nothing. As the great painter Sir Joshua Reynolds wrote: 'Invention, strictly speaking, is little more than a new combination which has previously been gathered and deposited in the memory; nothing can come of nothing.'

'He is most original who adapts from the most sources.'

Idea 2: Is it new in this context?

Everything has been thought of before, but the problem is to think of it again.

Johann Wolfgang von Goethe, German writer

You may think of an idea as being creative because it is new to *you*. But if this is the only criterion used, it is on the bottom rung of the ladder.

Case study: Spencer Penknives

Spencer Penknives, a long established Sheffield cutlery company, was going through hard times. Henry Parker, the managing director, came into the office one morning and summoned his senior executives. 'I was doing some creative thinking in the bath last night,' he said, 'and I've had a good idea.' An air of expectancy suddenly developed. 'We must ask our main customers why they aren't buying our products in such quantity now.'

A stunned silence followed. After the meeting on the way out, the sales director commented to a colleague, 'Some creative idea! We've been saying that for the last two years.'

Having an idea that is new to you is certainly a step in the right direction. But you must also ask yourself the following: Is it new to others? Has it been brought to market already?

In truth, it is virtually impossible to have a truly new idea. *Homo sapiens* has been on earth for a very long time. So almost anything you can conceive has probably been thought of or invented by someone else before.

Did you know that:

- ◆ Solomon's temple was protected by lightning rods?
- ◆ Emperor Nero devised a slot machine?
- ◆ Another Roman emperor had three elevators in his palace?

You can see what the author of *Ecclesiastes* meant when he coined the phrase 'there is nothing new under the sun'.

But some ideas may be born before their time. The Caesars, for example, may have had a few elevators, but the state of technology of their times meant that these could not be produced on any scale. Leonardo da Vinci may have sketched helicopters and submarines but, again, the technology for making and powering them wasn't available.

What is important is that an idea should be both relatively new and also feasible *in your given situation or environment*. For example, it's too late for you now – just as it was too early for Leonardo – to make your personal fortune from inventing the helicopter. That idea and its technology are no longer new.

Notice, incidentally, that whenever the tide of technology advances, especially if it makes a quantum leap like the advent of the internet, a whole range of 'old'/new ideas in the background of our collective memory suddenly become feasible. In other words, locked doors of opportunity slide open.

What's new?

Why do people *perceive* anything as new? They obviously won't do so if it's already familiar. The following questions point to the perception of newness in an idea or concept, product or service:

- Has it recently come into existence?
- Has it been made or used for only a short time?
- Is it freshly made ready for use, sale or circulation?
- Is it different from something similar that has existed before?
- Is it of superior quality?
- Has it just been thought of, manufactured or experienced?
- Has it recently been acquired?

You can now see that *new* is not the same as *original*, which, strictly speaking, applies only to something that is the first of its kind to exist. As most people's knowledge is inevitably limited, it's difficult to establish a claim to true originality. Research or enquiry will often unearth someone who has thought of your concept or product before.

> The concept of *newness* is a relative one: what may be new in one context is old in another.

Idea 3: What is innovation?

He that will not apply new remedies must accept new evils: for time is the greatest innovator.

Francis Bacon, English philosopher

An innovator is someone who introduces something new or as new, such as a product or service to a market. The concept includes improving an *existing* product or service.

Innovating means literally making new, thus altering or renewing. It doesn't mean conjuring something new out of thin air. The starting point is usually what is happening or how it is being done *now*.

As time goes by almost everything becomes obsolescent or obsolete. Indeed, after commenting on the pace of change today, a chief executive once said to me: 'If it works, it's obsolete.'

All our products and services stand in perennial need of renewal or replacement. The alternative to ignoring what Edmund Burke once called 'the great law of change' is a simple one: *you will go out of business*.

'Changing things is central to leadership.
Changing them before anyone else is creativeness.'

Idea 4: A community of creativity

The creative act thrives in an environment of mutual stimulation, feedback and constructive criticism – in a community of creativity.

William T. Brady, American businessman

You may find it useful to think of successful innovation as being comparable to the production of a play or film in which different people – say, a director, producer, author and scriptwriter – are involved. In successful innovation, one or more of the following individuals will be at work:

Role	Notes
Creative thinker	Has the power or quality to produce new ideas, especially those not currently in existence.
Innovator	Can bring in or introduce something new or as new, such as a product or service to the market. Also alters or makes changes to an established product or service.
Inventor	Comes up with a new and potentially commercial idea. Often combines both creative thinker and innovator.
Entrepreneur	Conceives or receives ideas and turns them into business realities. Often uses OPB (Other People's Brains) and OPM (Other People's Money) to develop a market opportunity.
Intrapreneur	Takes hands-on responsibility for creating innovation in any kind of organization. The intrapreneur may be the creator or inventor, but is always the dreamer who figures out how to turn an idea into profitable reality.
Champion	Picks up an idea, not necessarily his or her own, and runs with it. Shows commitment and tenacity in seeing it developed properly and successfully implemented.
Sponsor	Gives an idea the backing it deserves. Usually a senior manager who believes in it and influences key people to clear the way and help overcome obstacles as it is taken to realization.

Idea 5: Six barriers to creative thinking

One method of improving your creative thinking skills is to adopt an indirect or lateral strategy and attack obstacles that are hindering your approach. Here is an indicative – but no means exhaustive – list of the principal culprits:

1   *Negative attitude* – A tendency to focus on the negative aspects of problems and expend energy on worry, as opposed to seeking the opportunities inherent in a situation.

2   *Fear of failure* – A fear of looking foolish or being laughed at. Yet Tom Watson, founder of IBM, said: 'The way to accelerate your success is to double your failure rate.' Failure is a necessary condition of success.

3   *Executive stress* – Not having time to think creatively. An over-stressed person finds it difficult to think objectively at all. Unwanted stress reduces the quality of all mental processes.

4   *Following rules* – Some rules are necessary, but others encourage mental laziness. A tendency to conform to accepted patterns of belief or thought – the rules and limitations of the status quo – can hamper creative breakthroughs.

5   *Making assumptions* – A failure to identify and examine the assumptions you are making to ensure they are not excluding new ideas. Many *unconscious* assumptions, in particular, restrict thinking.

6   *Over-reliance on logic* – Investing all your intellectual capital in logical or analytical thinking – the step-by-step approach – can exclude imagination, intuition, feeling and humour.

Remember that the biggest barrier you will ever face is one particular belief about yourself, namely that you, almost alone among the human race, are not creative. This legacy of schools that focus too much on academic brilliance discourages creativity and forms a barrier that really stops people from even entering the race. It is a form of low self-esteem.

You were creative when you were a child, weren't you? Why not now? That child is still in you. Let it come out to play sometimes, and it will surprise you with its ideas. It will also reward you richly by keeping you forever young at heart.

> 'No matter how old you get, if you can keep the desire to be creative, you're keeping the child in you alive.'

Idea 6: Checklist for creativity and innovation

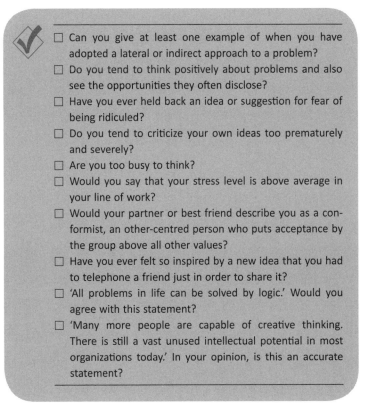

☐ Can you give at least one example of when you have adopted a lateral or indirect approach to a problem?

☐ Do you tend to think positively about problems and also see the opportunities they often disclose?

☐ Have you ever held back an idea or suggestion for fear of being ridiculed?

☐ Do you tend to criticize your own ideas too prematurely and severely?

☐ Are you too busy to think?

☐ Would you say that your stress level is above average in your line of work?

☐ Would your partner or best friend describe you as a conformist, an other-centred person who puts acceptance by the group above all other values?

☐ Have you ever felt so inspired by a new idea that you had to telephone a friend just in order to share it?

☐ 'All problems in life can be solved by logic.' Would you agree with this statement?

☐ 'Many more people are capable of creative thinking. There is still a vast unused intellectual potential in most organizations today.' In your opinion, is this an accurate statement?

Ten Greatest Ideas for How Your Mind Works

Idea 7: Inside your head

Every head is a world.

Cuban proverb

The physical base of your mind is of course your brain, the grey matter housed in your head. And what a wonder it is! Your brain is composed of about 10,000 million cells. In fact, it has more cells than there are people on the face of the earth! Each one of those cells can link up with approximately 10,000 of its neighbours, which gives you some 10,000 billion possible combinations.

Amazing, isn't it? But there's more:

◆ At any one moment your brain is receiving about 100 million pieces of information through your ears, eyes, nose, tongue and the touch receptors in your skin.

◆ Your brain consumes about 10 watts of power a day. If scientists tried to build a brain of silicon chips, they think it would need around one million times more power.

◆ If you were to stretch out all the nerve connections in your brain, they would reach a distance of about 3.2 million kilometres.

Three simple problems

See if you can solve these problems against the clock. Give yourself two minutes for each one. Here's a clue: a little bit of creative thinking is required in each case.

Problem 1: The nine dots

Take a piece of paper larger than this page and put on it a pattern of nine dots, like this:

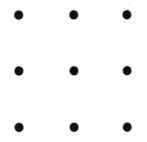

Now connect up the dots by four straight, consecutive lines (that is, without taking your pen or pencil off the paper). You should be able to complete this task within three minutes.

Problem 2: The six matchsticks

Place six matchsticks, preferably of the wooden variety, on a flat surface. Now arrange the matchsticks in a pattern of four equilateral (i.e. equal-sided) triangles. You may not break the matchsticks – that is the only rule.

Again, you should be able to do this within three minutes. There are at least two solutions, but I am asking you for the most elegant one.

Problem 3: The six coins

Six coins are arranged like this:

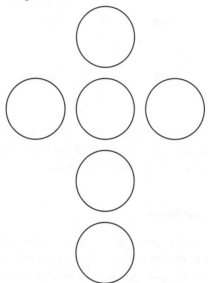

Move just one coin to another position so that you form two rows, *containing four coins each* when added up either horizontally or vertically.

If you have been unable to solve the three problems, ask yourself why you are having such difficulty.

Let me give you a further clue. The same principle that is preventing your mind from solving the problems is at work in all three instances.

Still baffled? Then turn to the Appendix for the answers an explanation of the principle involved.

A problem is a solution in disguise.

Idea 8: The mind at work

A picture is worth a thousand words.

Chinese proverb

When you are thinking to some purpose there are three principal mental functions at work:

1   *Analyzing* – resolving wholes into their constituent parts.
2   *Synthesizing* – building wholes out of their different elements
3   *Valuing* – judging or appraising on scales of relative worth.

These activities take place at various levels of the mind. Sometimes they submerge like a submarine into the *depth mind* (the unconscious) and resurface later on.

We think as whole persons, not as disembodied minds. Therefore *emotion* or feeling is ever present, or at least waiting in the wings. It plays a positive or negative role in the drama of thought.

Here, then, is a simple model of your mind at work:

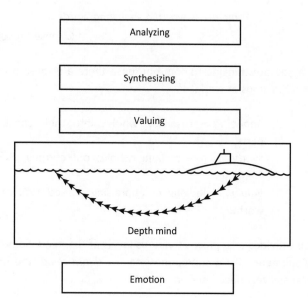

Idea 9: Analyzing, synthesizing and valuing

The three functions introduced in Idea 8 are not independent entities, they are locked together and interactive, like pieces in a jigsaw puzzle:

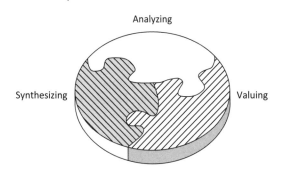

Functions of the Mind

Even so, we can discern some very distinctive differences between what each of the three functions does for us.

1 Analyzing

The word 'analyze' comes from the Greek verb meaning 'to loosen'. Its primary meaning is 'resolving into simple parts'. In other words, when I take my watch to pieces, I can strictly be said to be analyzing it.

The term, however, has overtones of meaning beyond this simple physical act. Indeed, the concept of 'loosening' does not imply a complete separation of elements. The knot tying two pieces of rope may be untied or merely loosened so that the nature of the knot can be understood.

Therefore analysis can be tracing things to their sources, and discovering general principles underlying concrete phenomena.

2 Synthesizing

Another word from the ancient Greeks, the first people in the world to think about thinking, synthesizing is the opposite of analyzing – it is 'the putting together of parts or elements so as to make up a complex whole'. Indeed, the Latin verb *cogito*, 'I think', can be derived from roots meaning 'to shake together'.

When the resulting whole is substantially new – especially if it is original – we describe the synthetic process as *creative*.

3 Valuing

The third major function of thinking, valuing is not finally reducible by or to analysis, or to synthesis, or to any combination of them.

Valuing, or thinking in relation to values or standards, should take its place beside analyzing and synthesizing as a major form of thinking in its own right.

It lies at the core of judgement and plays an essential role in all situations involving choices or decisions between options.

These major functions or modes of thought work together in our thinking. We are not usually conscious of the gear changes, yet the balance between them is changing from moment to moment. So one minute you may be primarily analyzing and the next valuing. They are complementary. Indeed, in all effective thinking – including the drama of creative thinking – all three functions are involved in a dynamic trio, although one actor may be on stage while the other two are waiting in the wings.

Avoid over-developing one function of the mind at the expense of the other two. It leads to a lopsided mind.

Have I ever suffered from 'paralysis by analysis'?
Can I think of any individual I have known well whom I would describe as having a tendency to be over-critical?

Idea 10: Decision making and problem solving

> *He who would lead must be a bridge.*
>
> Welsh proverb

Because the two slightly different processes of decision making and problem solving share a common internal structure, it has been possible for me to devise a model: *Crossing the River*.

If you come to a river you may be able to cross it yourself in some way, such as by jumping from one stepping stone to another. But if you want to take a *group* with all its impedimenta across the river, you must build a bridge:

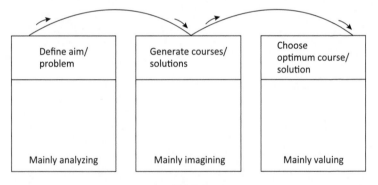

Crossing the river

As you will see, each of the phases of practical thinking draws mainly on one of the major functions. So it helps you to be able to separate them in your mind and also to see that all three are required in decision making or problem solving.

> You need skill in all three functions to be an effective thinker.

Idea 11: The depth mind in principle

The definition of genius is that it acts unconsciously; and those who have produced immortal works, have done so without knowing how or why. The greatest power operates unseen.

William Hazlitt

My own term for the creative unconscious – the *depth mind* – reflects the metaphor of the sea.

Imagining the sea and using it as an analogy allows us to observe the light of consciousness penetrating from the surface into the deeper 'caverns of the mind'. Gradually it becomes dimmer in the depths of 'no-man-fathomed', and below that it is lost in darkness.

The key point is that the three functions work on different levels of consciousness in the brain, often at the same time. Synthesizing, for example, can be done on a conscious level, as when assembling an electric plug or making a toy. But the process of putting together parts or elements to make a complex whole can also take place at an unconscious level. As English poet William Wordsworth wrote:

> *. . . there is a dark*
> *Inscrutable workmanship that reconciles*
> *Discordant elements, makes them cling together*
> *In one society.*

Many other creative people have reported as a fact that the welding of apparently disparate or diverse 'parts' into a pattern that is new (in the sense that the resultant whole has not been known before) takes place in the unconscious mind. The flash of inspiration, the sudden bright idea, is often the result of a period of subliminal mental activity.

> Can I think of an instance when a new thought or idea arose from my depth mind without any conscious volition on my part?

In fact, most people do experience at least some of the various products of our creative depth minds, such as *intuitions* (immediate perceptions or the mind working without reasoning), *hunches, premonitions* and *inklings*.

For creative thinkers, inklings (intimations of something as yet unknown) are especially important, for they may be signals that you are on the right track, even if your destination is still in the fog.

Idea 12: Checklist for listening to your depth mind

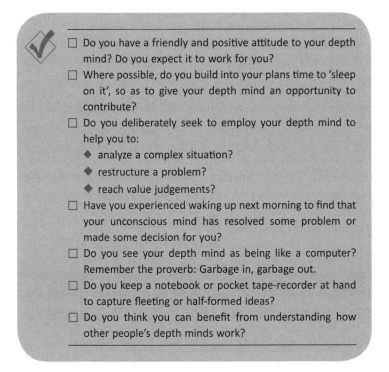

☐ Do you have a friendly and positive attitude to your depth mind? Do you expect it to work for you?

☐ Where possible, do you build into your plans time to 'sleep on it', so as to give your depth mind an opportunity to contribute?

☐ Do you deliberately seek to employ your depth mind to help you to:

◆ analyze a complex situation?

◆ restructure a problem?

◆ reach value judgements?

☐ Have you experienced waking up next morning to find that your unconscious mind has resolved some problem or made some decision for you?

☐ Do you see your depth mind as being like a computer? Remember the proverb: Garbage in, garbage out.

☐ Do you keep a notebook or pocket tape-recorder at hand to capture fleeting or half-formed ideas?

☐ Do you think you can benefit from understanding how other people's depth minds work?

Idea 13: The whole person thinks

Thought is not a trick, or an exercise, or a set of dodges
Thought is a man in his wholeness wholly attending.

D. H. Lawrence

Reason and emotion, thinking or feeling are often contrasted. It is not surprising, therefore, that thinking and feeling are intimately connected.

Emotion and motive come from the Latin verb *morere,* and both are ways of being moved. An emotion is a partly mental, partly physical response, the result of being stirred up by someone or something. Physical danger or threat, as we all know, produces a good example of emotion: a strong feeling of fear, accompanied by the kind of physiological changes that prepare your body for immediate and vigorous action. Fear or anxiety – fear without a specific object – is the principal cause of stress.

The two words emotion and feeling, one of Latin and one of Anglo-Saxon origin, can be distinguished from each other. *Emotion* carries a stronger implication of excitement and physical agitation than *feeling*, which suggests that our most powerful emotions lie dormant in the depths of our being and are only stirred up on rare occasions. Emotions are rather like strong winds, raging thunderstorms or blazing heat, while feelings are the more gentle breezes, showers and the slow warmth of sun on the skin.

Negative emotions or feelings, such as hatred or fear, anxiety or worry, can play havoc with all our thinking processes, but especially creative thinking. That is why the quality of calmness is so important if you want to think effectively. 'Reason and calm judgement,' wrote Roman historian Tacitus, 'the qualities especially belonging to a leader.'

To be an effective thinker and decision-maker you need to be able to control your emotions and feelings, not be controlled by them.

Yet positive feelings can enhance our intellectual powers. Love in particular is a great incentive to positive thinking. 'When love and skill unite,' said Emerson, 'expect a masterpiece.' And if it was without any feeling or interest, the mind would be like a computer without electricity, quite unable to work.

Sometimes dolphins lead mariners to safety. Sometimes, too, thinkers report the presence of a sensation of pleasure *before* they make a significant discovery – the kind of feelings that are the dolphins of the mind. Less poetically, psychologists call this phenomenon the *hedonic response*. Have you ever experienced it?

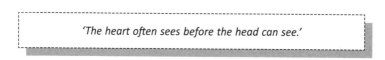

'The heart often sees before the head can see.'

Idea 14: Integrity

Integrity is the noblest possession.

Roman proverb

It is hard to over-emphasize the value of truth in any form of thinking, including creative thinking and innovation. If your new ideas and innovations are not based on truth, you are like the man who built his house on the shifting sands of mere novelty. That is why you need integrity to be a good thinker, for all kinds of effective thinking revolve around the sun of Truth.

Field Marshal Lord Slim once defined integrity by its effects: 'It is the quality which makes people trust you.' But what is it about your integrity that induces that feeling in others?

The word *integrity* literally means entireness, wholeness, soundness. An integer is a whole number. It is a holistic word. You might be tempted to conclude that integrity as such does not exist, or perhaps that it is the sum of all your moral qualities. For integrity suggests a unity that indicates interdependence of parts and the completeness or perfection of the whole.

Integrity implies an adherence to some set of moral, artistic or other values, spoken or unspoken, something outside yourself and especially Truth. It suggests, too, personal trustworthiness and incorruptibility to such a degree that you are incapable of being false to a trust or promise, responsibility or pledge.

> Can I identify a situation at work where I would be compelled to resign on grounds of conscience?
>
> Have I ever, in my career, refused to tell a lie and borne the consequences?
>
> Do I act as if I believe that truth is 'out there' when I am thinking?
>
> Do I think that the truth has a power or life of its own, that it will assert itself if only I allow it to do so?

Your ability as a practical thinker depends largely on your judgement, and judgement in turn is as much a function of your values and your valuing skills. It is an outcrop of your professional experience.

For a good leader truth is not only about factual accuracy, seeing reality as it is – although that is immensely important. It also spells trustworthiness, reliability and straightforwardness.

> *I never encourage deceit; and falsehood, especially if you have a bad memory, is the worst enemy a fellow can have. The fact is truth is your truest friend, no matter what the circumstances are.*

Abraham Lincoln, in a letter to
George E. Pickett, 22 February 1841

> 'Truth is great and shall prevail, when none care whether it prevail or not.'

Idea 15: Why integrity matters in innovation

In looking for people to hire, you look for three qualities: integrity, intelligence and energy. And if they don't have the first, the other two will kill you.

Warren Buffett, CEO, Berkshire Hathaway

As Warren Buffett wisely observes, you can hire intelligent, creative and innovative people, young people with bags of energy, fire and enthusiasm. They will come up with buckets of new ideas for products that they say will make you – and them – very rich. But if they lack integrity, if they cut their ethical corners, they could spell disaster for your organization.

People are inherently or innately moral. Therefore if you create or introduce practices or products that are immoral or unethical, you will be working against the grain of human nature. Short-term profits may be large, but sustainability – long-term success – will elude you.

Integrity without creativity may be barren, but creativity without integrity can produce monsters – think of the Nazi death camps. So make sure you seek out people who have integrity.

Idea 16: A clear conscience

A clear conscience never fears midnight knocking.

Chinese proverb

The depth mind is the seat of conscience, a rather specialized mental faculty that tells you – usually retrospectively or more helpfully in advance – that you have done or are about to do something that is *morally* wrong.

Far from it being a *bad* conscience, as it is sometimes called, it is a *good* conscience doing its proper work. Having a *clear* conscience – an outbox with no messages in it – means that you will sleep well in the Inn of Decision. Your depth mind won't wake you up or disturb you with bad dreams.

Whether or not you choose to respond to the first inklings of your conscience does have consequences. The dubious reward for ignoring what your conscience tells you is that its call will slowly dwindle to a whisper, and one day you will not even hear it at all. Your conscience will have atrophied.

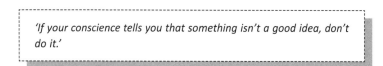

'If your conscience tells you that something isn't a good idea, don't do it.'

Seven Greatest Ideas for Developing Your Mind

Idea 17: Learning to trust your intuition

There is no logical way to the discovery of these elemental laws.
There is only the way of intuition, which is helped by a feeling
for the order lying behind the appearance.

Albert Einstein

Intuition is the most common general word for the faculty of the depth mind. It indicates the kind of comprehension or knowledge that comes quickly to awareness, apparently without the intervention of conscious reasoning, inferring or deliberation.

The most characteristic example of intuition is when you come to know, or suspect, that a situation exists when you have no direct evidence that it is the case.

Managers are often deterred from recognizing and using their own intuitive powers because they feel that somehow, intuition is not intellectually respectable. They certainly believe that it is not scientific enough. The cult of the rational manager has an iron grip on such minds. But this is nonsense. Some of the most celebrated scientists have been intuitive in their work.

If you are now inclined to be more aware and to give more status to intuition in thinking, you have already taken the first step towards making better use of it. The next step is to learn to trust your intuitive powers. That does not mean always, nor does it mean occasionally, because one cannot generalize about how often.

But you should be prepared to give your intuition the benefit of the doubt. You should build up a warm and friendly relationship to that part of your mind that is prepared to offer you this unique service.

Case study: Paul Getty

'When I first started drilling in the Oklahoma oil fields the consensus of expert judgement held that there could be no oil in the so-called Red Beds region. But like so many oilmen, I chose to temper all "analytical" thinking with a healthy dose of non-logical subjectivity. To me, the area looked as if it might hide oil. Largely on the basis of a hunch, I decided to see for myself. I began drilling in the Red Beds, struck oil and brought in a vast new producing field. I rather suspect that by relying upon such non-textbook thought processes and taking attendant risks, the biggest fortunes have been made – in oil and other endeavours.'

Business flair is a consistent theme in the lives of great industrialists and merchants. They can intuitively spot an opportunity for making money. They can smell a potential future profit where others can see nothing but present losses. It is an instinct that is separate from the dictates of reason or logic that guide more plodding minds. When it is not followed, such business people often realize their mistake only later.

Alfred Sloan once worked with William C. Durant, the founder of General Motors. He recalled that Durant 'would proceed on a course of action guided solely, as far as I could tell, by some intuitive flash of brilliance. He never felt obliged to make an engineering hunt for facts.' Sloan, perhaps the greatest manager of his day, concluded: 'The final act of business judgement is intuitive.'

'Intuition will tell the thinking mind where to look next.'

Idea 18: How intuitive are you?

The intuitive mind is a sacred gift and the rational mind is a faithful servant. We have created a society that humours the servant and has forgotten the gift.

Albert Einstein, German physicist

Intuition is awareness that a situation exists when reason or logic (if consulted) might say that it was improbable or even impossible for it to do so. Do you have such awareness:

Rarely	☐	Sometimes	☐
Frequently	☐	Never	☐

◆ In your judgement of people, do you tend to rely on first impressions? Are these usually right?

◆ Do you often 'feel' your way to a decision or to the solution for a problem?

◆ Do you sometimes find it difficult to explain your intuitions to others?

◆ When your intuitions turn out to be wrong, in hindsight why is this so?

Idea 19: Case study – Ludwig van Beethoven

Composers of genius have remarkable depth minds, albeit highly specialized ones. Other depth minds work in the same way, but seldom with such spectacular results!

What three facts can you learn about the depth mind from this description by German composer Beethoven (in *Thayer's Life of Beethoven*)?

> I carry my thoughts about with me for a long time, sometimes a very long time, before I set them down . . . At the same time my memory is so faithful to me that I am sure not to forget a theme which I have once conceived, even after years have passed. I make many changes, reject and reattempt until I am satisfied.
>
> Then the working-out in breadth, length, height and depth begins in my head, and since I am conscious of what I want, the basic idea never leaves me. It rises, grows upward, and I hear and see the picture as a whole take shape and stand forth before me as though case in a single piece, so that all that is left is the work of writing it down. This goes quickly, according as I have the time, for sometimes I have several compositions in labour at once, though I am sure never to confuse one with the other.
>
> You will ask me whence I take my ideas? That I cannot say with any degree of certainty: they come to me uninvited, directly or indirectly. I could almost grasp them in my hands, out in Nature's open, in the woods, during my promenades, in the silence of the night, at the earliest dawn.
>
> They are roused by moods which in the poet's case are transmuted into words, and in mine into tones, that sound, roar and storm until at last they take shape for me as notes.

Idea 20: Clear thinking

> *I keep six honest serving-men*
> *They taught me all I knew;*
> *Their names are What and Why and When*
> *And How and Where and Who.*
>
> Rudyard Kipling, English novelist

There is a link between having a good analytical mind and being a clear thinker. You have to be able to reduce a complex problem or situation to its essentials – analyzing – in order to be clear about it. That takes practice.

The way to improve your skills as a clear thinker is to challenge all that appears to be – in your own thinking or in the thought of others – *sloppy, inconclusive, blurred, confused, doubtful, foggy, fuzzy, muddled, obscure, unclear, unintelligible, vague*. You won't be short of work!

Notice what a major part asking the right questions plays in clear thinking. Indeed, sometimes finding the right question is more than half the answer. For starters, it is difficult to improve on Rudyard Kipling's famous six questions above. They are spanners of the mind that can loosen the most intractable of problems.

What you need is the ability to think for yourself, as if from first principles. That requires a balance of confidence and humility: confidence in your own intellectual powers and humility that keeps you from that fatal form of over-confidence known as arrogance.

 Can I call to mind three people I have met who had or have a reputation for their clear thinking?

Idea 21: Imagination

To raise new questions, new possibilities, to regard old problems from a new angle, requires creative imagination and marks real advance in science.

Albert Einstein, German physicist

Creativity is about having new ideas and innovation is about turning them into improved or new products and services. Both creativity and innovation call for imaginative thinking.

Imagination spans both the power of forming images of things once known but now absent, and the power of forming images of things not seen, or actually nonexistent, or incapable of actual existence.

In the first instance, imagination implies the use of memory as well as the image of power. In its second aspect, imagination usually suggests either a new combination of elements found in one's experience or an ability to conceive of something, seen only fragmentarily or superficially, as a complete, perfected and integral whole. As Shakespeare said, 'imagination bodies forth the forms of things unknown'.

Imagination is our sovereign gift. Without it we could not become aware of what the world might be. 'Imagination is everything,' as Einstein put it. 'It is the preview of life's coming attractions.'

> *'Imagination is the vision that sees possibilities in the materials and resources we have.'*

Idea 22: Holistic thinking

*I can see the whole of it at a single glance in my mind, as if it
were a beautiful painting or a handsome human being.*

Wolfgang Amadeus Mozart, Austrian composer

Sometimes decisions and solutions, intuitions and ideas seem to
grow in the mind. It is as if there is a grain of sand in the oyster that
grows into a pearl. It gives surprise and delight to the person fortunate enough to open it. Or think of it like a seed that falls on good
ground, sends down roots and grows in a holistic way.

The word *holistic*, incidentally, comes from the Greek *holos*, meaning
'whole'. It was coined in 1926 by the famous South African leader Jan
Smuts, who, apart from being a soldier and statesman, was also a
keen student of the agricultural sciences. He introduced it to describe
the tendency of Nature to produce wholes from the ordered group-
ings of units.

Babies are not parts that are assembled into a whole, they are wholes
which *grow* larger. That's how Nature works. By analogy our minds
work in the same way, some more so than others. Women, in my
opinion, tend to be more holistic than men. Perhaps they are closer
to Nature.

Holistic people tend to dislike too much analysis. Their pathway to
understanding a person or a situation is to listen to the *story* of how
they or it developed, from first beginnings to present state. The idea
of *growth* appeals to them. For example, 'growing' a business – not
just in size but in quality – may appeal to a holistic leader or entre-
preneur far more than making a lot of money.

Holistic people have a head start when it comes to creativity. By
contrast, at the other extreme of the spectrum come the *analysts*,
those who have over-developed that major function and equate it

with thinking. Famous physicist Neils Bohr once responded to a doctoral student's comment by saying: 'You are not thinking, you're merely being logical.'

Dissecting or taking things to bits, categorizing or classifying, useful though they can be, do not march so well under the creative banner. While they do have a part to play in the creative or innovative process, it's an ancillary one. Otherwise, as Wordsworth said, 'We murder to dissect.'

Knowing how to think holistically – to see the wood as well as the trees, to see the whole that is a sum of more than the constituent parts – is a key skill for an effective thinker.

Those who are good judges of people tend to have more holistic minds. People may have sets of qualities or strengths and weaknesses, but a psychological analysis of their traits seldom gives you a sense of knowing them. You are always dealing with a whole person.

Holistic minds tend to be attracted to the idea of growth. They like to help individuals and teams, organizations and communities, even nations, to grow to their full potential.

How do I plan to *grow* my business in the next three years?

Idea 23: Developing your thinking skills

Change fights ever on the side of those with practical wisdom.

Ancient Greek proverb

If you have read most of Part One you should have been able to focus your previous knowledge of your strengths and weaknesses – or rather, areas for improvement – as a thinker. As always, the principle is to build on your strengths and starve your weaknesses.

Case study: Lord Rothschild

'Often I feel frustrated when I am thinking about something,' said the scientist and banker Lord Rothschild, a Fellow of the Royal Society and first director of the British Government's 'Think Tank'. He was, he said, a good analyst, but not a truly creative thinker. 'Synthetic thinking, creative thinking if you like, is a higher order altogether. People who think creatively hear the music of the spheres. I have heard them once or twice,' he commented.

Rothschild is obviously correct in believing that we all have different profiles of strengths and weaknesses as thinkers. Creative thinkers are clearly stronger in synthesizing and in their imagination. But the best of them are equally strong in their analyzing ability and the faculty of valuing or judging. It is this combination of mental strengths, supported by some important personal qualities or characteristics, that makes for a formidable creative mind.

You will get nowhere in your self-development without feedback. It comes from two sources: life and other people. The former comes to you in the form of the consequences, both expected and unexpected, of the decisions you make. Reflect on these experiences in the light of the principles in this book, and learn your lessons well.

Exercise

Take a piece of paper and write down the feedback you have received from others about you as a thinker – I mean as both an effective thinker and also as a creative thinker. Is there a pattern in the comments you have received? What are your tendencies?

Who are the people who, by their example or their teachings, can help you to become more effective in this, the mental branch of leadership? Remember, all experienced leaders have something to teach you if you have a listening ear.

Humility is the name of the quality that keeps you always open to learn more. It is the necessary condition for excellence in leadership. And that same openness of mind is essential for you as a creative thinker.

Furthermore, recall the saying that humility is the only true wisdom by which we prepare our minds for all the possible changes of life.

 Am I willing to devote some time and effort to the problems I face? Do I see them not as problems but as opportunities to practise my skills as a thinker?

'There is no expedient to which a man will not resort to avoid the real labour of thinking.'

Sir Joshua Reynolds, English painter

Follow-up test

Creativity and innovation

☐ Have you a clear idea of the difference between creative thinking and innovation?

☐ Do you agree with the 'Newer is truer' school – that what is new is always superior to what is old?

☐ 'Life is a mixture of continuity and change.' What three things at work do you want to continue? What three things need changing?

☐ How far would you describe the organization where you work as a 'community of creativity'?

How your mind works

☐ Look again at the model in Idea 8. What elements would you subtract? What elements would you add?

☐ Have you developed a strong bias towards one of the three major functions or modes of thinking?

☐ Have you experience of your depth mind giving you intuitions, inklings, clues or ideas?

☐ Can you think of four people in history who showed considerable creativity but lacked integrity?

☐ Is your conscience your friend and your guide?

Developing your mind

☐ How did you learn to trust your intuition?

☐ 'Clear thinking is the companion to creative thinking.' Are your analytical faculties in good shape?

☐ 'Good design is clear thinking made visible.' Would you agree? Have you noticed three examples of that principle?

☐ What steps have you taken in the last two months to improve your powers of thought and imagination?

PART TWO

Developing Creative Intuition

Learning is like rowing upstream; not to advance is to drop back.

Chinese proverb

As a preliminary to tackling the more practical techniques and strategies for creative thinking later in the book, Part Two offers you a series of doors through which you can explore what it means to be a creative person.

The first cluster of Ideas revolves around the open-mindedness you need to develop. For without a wealth of information your mind will have no materials to work on. And without curiosity, the mind's natural eagerness to learn, the shelves in your larder will remain empty.

Being more creative is becoming childlike again, in the sense that you enjoy playing with ideas just for the fun of it. The second stream of Ideas invites you to rediscover your imagination. Experience, too, the joys of serendipity – creativity on holiday.

Therefore Part Two is concerned with your strategic or long-term future as a thinker, rather than tips or hints on how to solve a particular problem. If you don't invest in yourself, or rather your mind, your bank balance will slowly run down.

What farmer can expect harvest after harvest if he never puts some goodness back into the soil? Take a strategic or long-term approach to stocking or equipping your mind to do its work for you, especially if you have now identified creative management as one of your priorities.

Ten Greatest Ideas for Opening Your Mind

Idea 24: Curiosity

I have no exceptional talents, other than a passionate curiosity.

Albert Einstein, German physicist

'The important thing is not to stop questioning', said Einstein. 'Curiosity has its own reason for existing. One cannot help but be in awe when one contemplates the mysteries of eternity, of life, of the marvellous structure of reality. It is enough if one tries merely to comprehend a little of this mystery every day. Never lose a holy curiosity.'

Such curiosity is – or should be – the appetite of the intellect. Creative thinkers have it, because they need to be taking in information from many different sources. The novelist William Trevor, for example, sees his role as an observer of human nature: 'You've got to like human beings, and be very curious,' he says, otherwise he doesn't think it's possible to write fiction.

Of course, curiosity in this sense must be distinguished from the sort of curiosity that proverbially kills the cat. The latter implies prying into other people's minds in an objectionable or intrusive way, or meddling in their personal affairs. True curiosity is simply the eager desire to learn and know. Such disinterested intellectual curiosity can become habitual. Leonardo da Vinci's motto was 'I question'.

Case Study: Napoleon on HMS *Bellerophon*

If you or I had been in French Emperor Napoleon's shoes after his shattering defeat at Waterloo, we might well have lapsed into a state of inward-looking depression, if not despair. Not so Napoleon. Following his defeat he abdicated, with the apparent intention of going into exile in America.

At Rochefort, however, he found the harbour blockaded and he decided to surrender himself to the English Royal Navy. He was escorted aboard HMS *Bellerophon*. It was a new experience for him to see the inside of a ship of the Royal Navy, the instrument of France's defeat at Trafalgar a few years earlier.

An English eyewitness on board noticed that 'he is extremely curious, and never passes anything remarkable in the ship without immediately demanding its use, and inquiring minutely into the manner thereof'.

'Curiosity in children is but an appetite for knowledge,' wrote the philosopher John Locke. You should aim to retain throughout your life that eager desire to see, learn or know. Curiosity is the mind on tiptoe. Creative thinkers tend to have a habit of curiosity that leads them to give searching attention to whatever interests them.

> Thinking is a way of trying to find things out for yourself. If you always blindly accepted what others told you, there would be nothing to be curious about.

One way to develop your curiosity is to begin to ask more questions, both when you are talking with others and when you are talking to yourself in your mind. Questioning, carefully done, helps you to distinguish between what is known and what is unknown.

Akio Morita, co-founder of the Sony corporation, once said in an interview, 'My chief job is to constantly stir or rekindle the curiosity of people that gets driven out by bureaucracy and formal schooling systems.' Being continually curious is what makes a good manager.

Curiosity is one of the permanent and certain characteristics of a vigorous intellect.

Samuel Johnson, *English lexicographer*

Idea 25: Listen for ideas

Listening requires more intelligence than speaking.

Turkish proverb

'You hear not what I say to you,' says the Lord Chief Justice to Shakespeare's Falstaff. 'Very well, my Lord, very well,' replies the irrepressible old rogue. 'Rather, if you will excuse me, it is the disease of not listening, the malady of not marking, that I am troubled with.'

Poor listening ability is a common affliction, but creative thinkers do not suffer from it. Although we know very little about Falstaff's creator, we can at least surmise with some confidence that he was a good listener.

What constitutes such a rare beast as a good listener? First, a good listener will have curiosity, that all-essential desire to learn. That requires a degree of humility, the key to having an open mind. For if you think you know it all, or at least if you believe you know more than the person to whom you are talking, you are hardly inclined to listen. Hitler was an appallingly bad listener for that very reason.

Having an open mind does not guarantee that you will buy the idea, proposition or course of action being put to you. But it does mean that you are genuinely in the marketplace for new ideas. You will buy if the price is right.

The next requirement is to control your analytical and critical urges. Your first priority is to grasp fully what the other person is actually saying, especially if it is a new and therefore strange idea to you.

Do you have a clear picture of it in your mind? A hearer only hears what someone is saying; a listener discovers the real importance of the other person's words.

The act of comprehension, then, should come before the process of analysis and valuation. Until you are clear about what is being said or suggested, you are in no position either to agree or to accept.

A good listener is creative in the sense that he or she draws the best out of you. All professional musicians will tell you that the audience plays a vital part in a performance. Referring to a play that had recently failed, Irish writer Oscar Wilde said: 'The play was a great success, but the audience was a disaster.'

Case study: Lord Thomson of Fleet

One of the most creative listeners I have come across was Roy Thomson. In his autobiography, *Long After Sixty*, he had this to say about his policy of being a good listener:

> I am always curious, always hopeful . . . The way I look at it, everyone has an idea and one in a dozen may be a good idea. If you have to talk to a dozen people to get one good idea, that isn't wasteful work. People are continually passing things on to me, because I have given them to believe that I will be interested, I might even pay for it! Sometimes, usually when it is least expected, something comes up that is touched with gold.

Roy Thomson was full of questions on every subject. His interest was like a perennial spring: it flowed from the hope that the companion of the moment might add information to some current concern, or even reveal some world that Roy had not so far entered.

Go round asking a lot of damfool questions and taking chances. Only through curiosity can we discover opportunities, and only by gambling can we take advantage of them.

Clarence Birdseye, *American industrialist*

Idea 26: Reading to generate ideas

The use of reading is to aid us in thinking.

Edward Gibbon, English historian

'I love to lose myself in other men's minds,' wrote English essayist Charles Lamb. 'When I am not walking, I am reading; I cannot sit and think. Books think for me.'

For many people, reading and research are more devices for avoiding thought rather than aids to it. But reading for diversion or entertainment, or reading merely for information, is different from reading for idea generation. What kinds of reading will develop your creative imagination?

Good fiction may come high on your list. Novelist John Fowles said that the reader of fiction has to take part and do half the work. 'I like the vagueness of the printed word,' he said. Take a sentence like 'She walked across the road.' You have to imagine the situation, so you have freedom to picture it in the way you want.

No two people have ever imagined Tolstoy's characters in *War and Peace* in the same way. This makes for richness in reading, since it involves a communion between author and reader. Prose and poetry will never die.

The words of Francis Clifford, writer of 15 novels, apply to all books likely to be useful to a creative thinker:

> *A writer's task is not to spell everything out. It is really to imply and infer and hint, to give the reader the opportunity of total involvement by encouraging him or her to contribute his or her own reflections and imagery.*

Exercise

Go to your nearest public library with a friend and find the main nonfiction section. Ask your friend to blindfold you and to guide you round the shelves. Select any three books at random. At home, list the core ideas in each book; not more than five in each instance.

Reading books – not just this one! – can stimulate and develop your powers of creative thinking. If nothing else, a good book can put you into a working mood.

If you are resolved to devote as much time and attention to your mental fitness as the average person spends on that more wasting asset, the human body, why not explore the world of books?

Idea 27: Creative reading

A good reader also creates.

Swiss proverb

'Some books are to be tasted, others to be swallowed and some few to be chewed and digested,' wrote Tudor philosopher Francis Bacon. Reading without reflecting has been compared to eating without digesting. One page or even one paragraph properly digested will be more fruitful than a whole volume hurriedly read. Or, as the film mogul Sam Goldwyn said to a hopeful author, 'I have read part of your book all the way through.'

Reading books can stimulate and develop your powers of creative thinking. Did you know, for example, that:

- Hindus used the cowpox virus centuries before Jenner?
- the reaping machine was described as a 'worn-out French invention' in the sixteenth century?
- a thousand years before Christ, the Chinese extracted digitalis from living toads to treat heart disease, recorded earthquakes undetected by the human senses, and used an instrument that always pointed north?

Some books will stimulate your creativity more than others. Naturalist Charles Darwin once declared:

If I had my life to live over again, I would have made a rule to read some poetry and listen to some music at least once a week; for perhaps the parts of my brain now atrophied would thus have been kept active through use. The loss of these tastes is a loss of happiness, and may possibly be injurious to the intellect, and more probably to the moral character, by enfeebling the emotional part of our nature.

Creative thinkers tend to read widely. Books are storehouses of ideas, thoughts, facts, opinions, descriptions, information and dreams. Some of these, removed from their setting, may connect to your present or future interests as a thinker.

'Reading furnishes the mind only with materials of knowledge; it is thinking that makes what we read ours,' wrote philosopher John Locke.

'Reading is to the mind what exercise is to the body.'

Idea 28: Keep a notebook

A commonplace book contains many notions in garrison, whence the owner may draw out an army into the field on competent warning.

Thomas Fuller, English scholar and preacher

'The horror of that moment,' the King went on, 'I shall never, *never* forget!' 'You will, though,' the Queen said, 'If you don't make a memorandum of it.' This advice from Lewis Carroll in *Alice in Wonderland* certainly applies in the field of creative thinking.

One practical step you can take now is to buy a new notebook to record possible materials for your present or future use: ideas, a scrap of conversation, something seen or heard on television or radio, a quotation from an article or a book, an observation, a proverb. Write it down!

You have probably had the experience of waking up in the middle of the night with an idea. It was such a good one that you told yourself to remember it the next morning. But, like the memory of your dreams, it fades fast away.

'Every composer knows,' Hector Berlioz said, 'the anguish and despair occasioned by forgetting ideas which one has not had time to write down.' He spoke from experience, he added.

Keep a pencil and pad by your bed. Carry a pocket notebook so that ideas that strike you while you're waiting for someone or travelling on a train can be recorded. Later you can transfer these jottings to your main notebook.

Apart from reinforcing and extending your memory, the practice of keeping a commonplace book of notable passages or quotations in particular has one fairly obvious further benefit. The labour of copying them out gives you occasion to reflect deeply on them.

As you slowly write or type, you have to pay attention to both the exact form and the content of what is being said. The act of writing impresses the words more deeply on your mind. Once a thought is in your own handwriting you have appropriated it personally: it is now numbered among the ideas and influences that matter to you.

> ' "A person who can create ideas of note," said Japanese industrialist Konosuke Matsushita, "is a person who has learned much from others." Always look on the people you meet as your potential teachers.'

Idea 29: A useful tool for creative thinking

Genius is the capacity for seeing relationships where lesser men see none.

William James

There are two important principles when keeping a commonplace notebook as a tool for creative thinking:

1 *Don't try to be systematic* – Put down entries in the order in which they occur to you. Give a short title to the entry, and perhaps a date. Don't try to be too systematic, by putting everything on cards or looseleaf paper arranged alphabetically, indexed and cross-indexed. If you are a scientist, for example, that may be the right method. But that is not the best way when it comes to developing your powers as a creative thinker.

2 *Follow your instinct* – The second principle is to let your instinct or intuitive sense decide what you think is worth noting down. Include whatever impresses you as stimulating, interesting or memorable. At this stage it doesn't matter too much if the idea is right or wrong, only that it is interesting.

Later – months later – you may need to do some editing, but initially what matters is whether or not the prospective entry gives you a spontaneous reaction of excitement or deep interest. As Shakespeare wrote: 'No profit grows where is no pleasure taken.'

In this form your commonplace notebook is a very useful tool for creative thinking on a variety of subjects that concern you. This method brings together some very diverse material.

When you look through your notebook you will begin to notice various constellations of links and connections. It is this coming together of elements hitherto unrelated – the interaction of unlikely bedfellows – that makes a notebook of this nature a veritable seedbed of new ideas.

- ◆ Use hardcover books, but not large or bulky ones. Ledgers are too heavy to carry around.
- ◆ Leave a large margin and plenty of space above and below, so that you can add some notes in pencil later. The margin can also be used for cross-referencing.
- ◆ You may like to write with different coloured inks, perhaps to distinguish different subjects.
- ◆ Number the pages and then you can add a simple index at the front by subject and with a page reference

You need to give your depth mind time to work, so I suggest that you do not look at your entries too often.

In my experience, the best time to browse through them creatively (unless, that is, you are hunting for a reference for a specific purpose) is on a train or air journey, waiting in airports, or on holiday when your mind is fresh and unencumbered with daily business.

Idea 30: Your own ideas bank

Many ideas grow better when transplanted into another mind than in the one where they sprung up.

Oliver Wendell Holmes, US judge

Keeping a notebook is more than a useful habit: it is a vitally important tool for all creative thinking purposes.

'A man would do well to carry a pencil in his pocket,' wrote the philosopher Francis Bacon, 'and write down the thoughts of the moment. Those that come unsought are commonly the most valuable and should be secured, because they seldom return.'

Writing down a quotation or passage, fact or piece of information is a means of meditating on it and appropriating it personally so that it grows into part of you.

Imagine that your notebook is like a kaleidoscope. At a time when you are feeling in a creative frame of mind, give it a metaphorical shake. You can play with new combinations and interconnections – they may suggest new ideas or lines of thought.

Don't forget to add inspirational quotations, stories and examples to your own personal collection. For creative thinking calls for stimulus, encouragement and inspiration. If you build a positive orientation of mind, you will become increasingly more creative in your thinking.

The philosopher Thomas Hobbes kept a notebook at hand. 'As soon as a thought darts,' he said, 'I write it down.'

Follow up an idea promptly. Once, when scientist Isaac Newton had a particularly illuminating idea while walking down the steps of his wine cellar to fetch a bottle for some guests, he promptly abandoned his errand. The bemused guests discovered him some time later hard at work in his study!

Three ways to fill your ideas bank

1 Curiosity

◆ Curiosity is essentially the eager desire to see, learn or know. It is the mind on tiptoe.

◆ Creative thinkers tend to have a habit of curiosity that leads them to give searching attention to what interests them.

◆ Thinking is a way of trying to find out for yourself. If you always knew where it was taking you there would be nothing to be curious about.

2 Observation

◆ The ability to give careful, analytical and honest attention to what you see is essential. If you don't notice and observe, you will not think.

◆ Observation implies attempting to see a person, object or scene as if you had never seen it before in your life.

◆ The act of observation is not complete until you have recorded what you have seen, thereby helping to commit it to memory.

3 Listening

◆ A childlike curiosity and an open mind, backed up by sharp analytical skills and sensitive judgement, are the essential prerequisites for being a good listener.

◆ Your priority must always be to achieve a grasp of the nature and significance of what is being said to you. Ask questions to elicit its full meaning. Understanding comes before evaluation.

◆ Listen out for ideas, however incomplete and ambiguous, as well as for potentially relevant facts and information.

Idea 31: Suspend judgement

Criticism often takes from the tree caterpillars and blossoms together.

Jean-Paul Sartre, French author

Suspending judgement in terms of my model of the mind at work (see Idea 8) means erecting a temporary and artificial barrier between the analyzing and synthesizing faculties of your mind on the one hand, and the valuing faculty on the other.

We tend to critically evaluate our own ideas – or half ideas – far too soon. Criticism, especially the wholly negative kind, can be like a cold, white frost in spring: it kills off seeds and budding leaves. If you can relax your quick-on-the-trigger self-critical responses and let newborn ideas have some room to breathe, you will become a more productive thinker.

Johann Schiller, the celebrated German poet who trained as a lawyer, then became a military surgeon and ended his career as professor of history at Jena in 1788, once wrote to a friend:

The reason for your complaint (about not being creative) lies, it seems to me, in the constraint which your intellect imposes upon your imagination.

Here I will make an observation, and illustrate it by an allegory. Apparently, it is not good – and indeed it hinders the creative work of the mind – if the intellect examines too closely the ideas already pouring in, as it were, at the gates.

Hence your complaints of unfruitfulness, for you reject too soon and discriminate too severely.

Withdraw the guards from the gates of your mind. Let ideas rush in. Don't reject too soon and discriminate too severely. Only then, when they have settled down, can you review and examine them completely.

Idea 32: Choose your thinking companions carefully

To find fault is easy; to do better may be difficult.

Plutarch, Greek historian

Surround yourself with people who are not going to subject your ideas to premature criticism. 'I can achieve that easily by not talking about them,' you might reply. Yes, but that cheats you out of the kinds of discussion that are generally valuable to thinkers.

These fall under the general principle that 'two heads are better than one'. It is useful to hear another person's perspective on the problem. They may have relevant experience or knowledge. They are likely to spot and challenge your unconscious assumptions. They can lead you to question your preconceptions and what you believe are facts.

In short, you need other people in order to think – thinking is a social activity – but you don't need over-critical people, or those who cannot reserve their critical responses in order to fit in with your needs.

That is the main reason why you should be cautious about sharing your seedling ideas with others whom you do not know too well. Some people are born critics!

There is a Chinese saying about such a person: 'He could find fault with a bird on the wing.'

The negative critic is like an underwater fisherman equipped with a gun and various darts, deadly phrases that he launches at any fish he sees stirring in your depth mind, such as:

- ◆ 'We tried that before.'
- ◆ 'Let's get back to reality.'

- 'I don't like the idea.'
- 'Good idea in theory, but impractical.'
- 'You'll make us a laughing stock.'
- 'Where did you dig that one up from?'
- 'It's never been tried before.'
- 'It won't work here.'
- 'It can't be done.'
- 'We've always done it this way.'
- 'It costs too much.'

A true or constructive critic, in contrast, might be defined as one who expresses a reasoned opinion on any matter involving a judgement of its value, such as truth, beauty or technical quality.

This sort of critic appreciates the value that is already there. The constructive part comes into play when such a critic suggests ways in which value can be added to the idea or matter under scrutiny. They build on your ideas.

When it comes to trying to think about fresh possibilities, there are two kinds of people. The first, when confronted with a new idea, will react in a distinctly negative way. By clear, logical thinking they may soon be able to show that the idea is wrong or that the plan is unworkable. The second type will react differently. They will toy with it, and speculate what the implications might be if the idea could be put into practice. Because of the novelty of the proposal, their impulse is to wish it could be shown to be true.

A condition of creativity seems to be a readiness to side with, empathize with and explore the possibilities of fresh ideas. It also seems to be compatible with the attitude of discriminating criticism previously discussed. This openness in fact consists of vigorous attention to ideas which, because they are important, merit criticism in the interests of their refinement or extension.

It is one of the offices of a friend, if no one else, to offer you constructive criticism about your work and perhaps also about your personal conduct. If we did not have this form of feedback, we should never improve. But there is a time and a place for everything – and that time is *not* when you are exploring and experimenting with new ideas. This is the reason professional creative thinkers – authors, inventors and artists, for example – seldom like to talk about work in progress.

> Neither praise nor blame is the object of true criticism. Justly to discriminate, firmly to establish, wisely to prescribe and honestly to be aware – these are the true aims and duties of criticism.

As a generalization, some social climates in families, working groups or organizations encourage and stimulate creative thinking, while others stifle or repress it. The latter tend to value analysis and criticism above originality and innovative thinking.

Premature criticism from others can kill off the seeds of creative thinking. Besides managing your own critical faculty, you have to turn the critical faculties of others to good account. That entails knowing when and how to avoid criticism as well as when and how to invite it.

Idea 33: Negative capability

Negative Capability, that is when man is capable of being in uncertainties, mysteries, doubts, without any irritable reaching after fact and reason.

John Keats, English poet

These words of the poet John Keats point to an important attribute. It was, he felt, the supreme gift of William Shakespeare as a creative thinker. It is also important, he added, for all creative thinkers to be able 'to remain content with half-knowledge'. Philosopher Francis Bacon echoes the same thought but adds a note of hope: 'If a man begins with certainties,' Bacon wrote, 'he shall end in doubts; but if he will be content to begin with doubts he will end with certainties.'

By temperament, some people find any sort of uncertainty or doubt uncomfortable and even stressful. They jump to conclusions or decisions – any certainties – just to escape from the unpleasant feeling of being not certain, undecided, in the fog of doubt. They are like the young man who will not wait to meet the right girl, however long the waiting, but marries the first available, simply in order to escape from the state of being unmarried.

The great American pioneer Daniel Boone, famous for his journeys into the trackless forests of the Western Frontier in the region we now call Kentucky, was once asked if he ever got lost. 'I can't say I was ever lost,' he replied slowly, after some reflection, 'but I was once sure bewildered for three days.'

As a creative thinker you may never quite feel lost, but you will certainly be bewildered for long stretches of time.

Creative thinking often, although not always, does require an untiring patience. Secrets aren't yielded easily. You have to be willing if necessary to persist in your particular enterprise of thought, despite counter-influences, opposition or discouragement. And it's tough. 'I think and think, for months, for years,' said Albert Einstein, 'Ninety-nine times the conclusion is false. The hundredth time I am right.'

So develop negative capability, your capacity to live with doubt and uncertainty over a sustained period. 'One doesn't discover new lands,' said French novelist André Gide, 'without consenting to lose sight of the shore for a very long time.'

'The last key in the bunch is often the one to open the lock.'

Fourteen Greatest Ideas for Thinking Outside the Box

Idea 34: Practise serendipity

One sometimes finds what one is not looking for.

Sir Alexander Fleming, discoverer
of the medical uses of penicillin

Serendipity is a happy word. Horace Walpole coined it to denote the faculty of making unexpected and delightful discoveries by accident. In a letter to a friend (28 January 1754) he says that he formed it from the title of a fairy story, *The Three Princes of Serendip* (an ancient name for Sri Lanka), for the princes 'were always making discoveries, by accidents and sagacity, of things they were not in quest of'.

If serendipity suggests chance, finding things of value when we are not actually looking for them, the finder must at least be able to see the creative possibilities of their discovery. Edison was seeking something else when he came across the idea of the mimeograph, a duplicator. He had the good sense to realize that he had made a discovery of importance and soon found a use for it.

Exercise

With hindsight it is often easier to see the effects of serendipity in your life. Looking back, can you identify three occasions when you made important discoveries, or met key people in your life's story, when you were not expecting to do so?

Serendipity goes against the grain of narrow-focus thinking, where you concentrate your mind on an objective or goal to the exclusion of all else. It invites you to have a wide span of attention, wide enough to notice something of significance even though it is apparently irrelevant or useless to you at present.

The three princes in Walpole's story were travellers. Explorers into the unknown often make unexpected discoveries. As the proverbial schoolchild knows, Christopher Columbus was seeking a new sea route to Asia when he discovered the New World. He thought he had reached India, which is why he called the natives he found there Indians.

When you travel – literally or figuratively – you should do so in a serendipitous frame of mind. Expect the unexpected. You may not discover America, but you will have some happy and unexpected 'finds'.

When you are thinking you are always travelling mentally, you are on a journey. For genuine thinking is always a process possessing direction or purpose. You may not always know where you are going, but you do know that you are trying to take yourself and others forwards.

Look out for the unexpected thoughts, however lightly they stir in your mind. Sometimes an unsuspected path or byway of thought that opens up might be more rewarding than following the fixed route you had set yourself.

 Can I think of an occasion when I made a discovery that I was not actually looking for?

Idea 35: The art of making discoveries by accident

Fortune brings in some boats that are not steered.

William Shakespeare

Serendipity means finding valuable and agreeable ideas or things – or people – when you are not consciously seeking them.

You are more likely to be serendipitous if you have a wide span of attention and a broad range of interests. Above all, you need an open mind and a degree of curiosity.

Being over-organized, planning your life down to the last minute like a control freak, is inimical to creativity. For chaos often breeds ideas. As creator of Winnie-the-Pooh A. A. Milne once said: 'One of the advantages of being disorderly is that one is constantly making exciting discoveries.' Don't be an over-controller of your own mind.

The lack of expert or specialized knowledge in a given field is no bar to being able to make a creative contribution. Indeed, too much knowledge may be a disadvantage. As statesman Disraeli said, we must 'learn to unlearn'.

Developing your capacity for creative thinking will bring you rewards, but they may not be the ones you were expecting. Don't refuse unexpected gifts or insist always on having things your way.

A creative thinker needs to be adventurous and open-minded like a resourceful explorer. You do not actually know what is around the next corner, even though you think you do. Sometimes in life you never quite know what you are looking for until you find it. Living fully calls for imagination as well as brains, which is why we have been given this faculty.

Idea 36: Chance favours the prepared mind

Where observation is concerned, chance favours only the prepared mind.

Louis Pasteur, French chemist
and inventor of pasteurization

What does it mean for you to have a prepared mind? You have to be purposeful in that you are seeking an answer or solution to some problem. You have become exceptionally sensitive to any occurrence that might be relevant to that search. You have the experience to recognize and interpret a clue when you see or hear one. That entails the ability to remain alert and sensitive for the unexpected while watching for the expected.

Case study: Sir Alastair Pilkington

Before the development of the float process by a research team led by Sir Alastair Pilkington, glass-making was labour intensive and time consuming, mainly because of the need to grind and polish surfaces to get a brilliant finish.

Pilkington's proprietary process eliminated this final manufacturing stage by floating the glass, after it is cast from a melting furnace, over a bath of molten tin about the size of a tennis court.

The idea for 'rinsing' glass over a molten tin bath came to Sir Alastair when he stood at his kitchen sink washing dishes. The float process gives a distortion-free glass of uniform quality with bright, fire-polished surfaces. Savings in costs are considerable. A float line needs only half the number of workers to produce three times as much glass as with the old production methods.

Case study: Charles Goodyear

Charles Goodyear discovered the vulcanization of rubber in 1839 by similar observation of a chance event. He had been experimenting for many years to find a process for treating crude or synthetic rubber chemically to give it such useful properties as strength and stability, but without success. One day as he was mixing rubber with sulphur he spilt some of the mixture on top of a hot stove. The heat vulcanized it at once. Goodyear immediately saw the solution to the problem that had baffled him for years.

As Goodyear pointed out, however, chance was by no means the only factor in his useful discovery. He said:

> I was for many years seeking to accomplish this object, and **allowing nothing to escape my notice** that related to it. Like the falling apple before Newton's gaze, it was suggestive of an important fact to one whose mind was previously prepared to draw an inference from **any occurrence which might favour the object of his research**. While I admit that these discoveries of mine were not the result of scientific chemical investigation, I am not willing to admit that they are the result of what is commonly called accident. I claim them to be the result of **the closest application and observation**.

I have put some of Goodyear's words into bold because they highlight the importance of having a wide focus of attention and keen powers of observation. His message is admirably summed up in Pasteur's famous words which bear repetition: 'In the field of observation, chance favours only the prepared mind.'

Notice that you will have to be willing to invest a good deal of time in fruitless work, for opportunities in the form of significant clues do not come often. In those long hours, experiment with new procedures. Expose yourself to the maximum extent to the possibility of encountering a fortunate accident. And, above all, keep your eyes open.

Idea 37: Be open-minded and receptive

*The real magic of discovery lies not in seeking new landscapes
but in having new eyes.*

Marcel Proust, French novelist

If you wish to develop your power to generate new ideas, the importance of having an open mind and a degree of curiosity stands out
clearly. You have to continually ask yourself questions about what is
happening around you – and be ready for surprising answers.

'I roamed the countryside searching for answers to things I did not
understand,' Leonardo da Vinci tells us. Among the questions that
preoccupied him was 'why birds sustain themselves in flight'. It was
the right question to ask. Eventually the pursuit of it led to our human
conquest of the air and, many centuries later, the formulation of the
laws of aerodynamics.

Things that happen apparently by chance, without any human
intention or observable cause, can acquire a sudden or gradual significance for an alert, open and receptive mind.

- ◆ The sweetening effect of saccharine, for example, was
  accidentally discovered by a chemist who happened to
  eat his lunch in the laboratory without washing his hands
  after some experiments.
- ◆ Ira W. Rufel provides another example. He observed the
  effects when a feeder failed to place a sheet of paper in
  a lithograph machine, and the work on the printing
  surface left its full impression on the printing cylinder.
  This led him to invent the offset method of printing.

Fruitful accidents tend to happen to those who, so to speak, deserve
them. Don't wait for them, but learn to be aware and awake when
they happen.

To see and recognize a clue in such unexpected events demands an open-minded sensitivity as well as skills of observation. To interpret the clue and realize its possible significance requires a mind without preconceptions, imaginative thinking, the habit of reflecting on unexpected observations – and some original flair. Yes, and a dash of luck.

> A closed mind is tight, rigid, hierarchical and tunnel visioned. By contrast, an open mind is more relaxed, receptive, exploratory, democratic, humorous and playful. Which do I prefer?

Idea 38: The untrapped mind

The 'untrapped mind' is open enough to see many possibilities, humble enough to learn from anyone and everything, perceptive enough to see things as they really are, and wise enough to judge their true value.

Konosuke Matsushita, Japanese industrialist

A trap is a contrivance of some kind for catching animals. To be in a trap is to be in a cage, like a song bird who cannot fly. An untrapped mind is one that is free to move, free to fly like a lark in the sky. It is 'in the clear'.

Famous as an outstanding Japanese business leader, Matsushita was a passionate believer in the merits of having such a mind. He identifies four of its qualities:

1 Openness – being responsive to a wide range of possibilities, new ideas, suggestions and opportunities.
2 Humility – being ready to learn from anyone, regardless of their status, and everything, failures and disappointments as well as successes.
3 Perceptive – being able to see with a clear eye things, people and ideas as they really are.
4 Wisdom – integrating one's judgement of value with one's clear thinking and creative orientation.

Can I identify a manager who works in my organization at present who consistently shows openness of mind, humility, perceptiveness and practical wisdom?

There is a Polish proverb about humility: 'The humble calf drinks the milk of two cows.' In other words, a creative person, one with an 'untrapped mind', will not be too fussy. They will range widely, and will acquire and adapt ideas from more than one source.

Idea 39: The holistic mind at work

When spiders' webs unite, they can tie up a lion.

Ethiopian proverb

The essential principle of holism in nature is that the whole is always greater than the parts. If you have a holistic mind, you can see the whole wood and not just a collection of trees. All living things are wholes. Parts working together in a whole have a synergy that is greater than the energy of the parts individually considered.

Look at a candle flame. Why does it keep approximately the same size and shape while it's flickering? In this case, the 'parts' are flows of vaporized wax, oxygen and burnt gases. The processes of combustion and diffusion give the interaction between these flows, and these interactions show us at what size and shape the flame will be approximately stable.

The strength of a rope is another example of a holistic property. This strength is a result of interaction among the individual strands, caused by twisting. With the strands untwisted, the rope's strength is governed by the weakest strand; twisted, the strands act together and increase their strength.

A holistic mind therefore has a special way of looking at things or people, at the world itself. It is not eager to take things to bits at first glance. Rather, it waits to see the full pattern, the whole – the wood rather than the trees. Equal mental weight is given to the whole in relation to the parts, hence a certain reluctance to dismember it. If a cruel schoolboy pulls the legs and wings off a fly he is left with a dead fly: the parts are there but the whole is gone.

Thinkers such as Albert Einstein exemplify this union of formidable powers of analysis with a strain of holistic thinking that seeks out the simple or whole.

> How can I strengthen my tendency to think holistically about people and problems?

Werner Heisenberg, one of the fathers of quantum physics, once spoke to Einstein of the 'almost frightening simplicity and wholeness of the relationships which nature suddenly spreads out before us'.

This theme of simplicity, wholeness and beauty – revealed through mathematical formula or detailed experimentation – recurs again and again as Nature's mysteries are explored.

There is definitely a family relationship between imagination and holistic thinking. Take as an example this description of the crucial phase in composition by one of the world's great composers, Wolfgang Amadeus Mozart:

> *First bits and crumbs of the piece come and gradually join together in my mind; then the soul getting warmed to the work, the thing **grows** more and more, and I spread it out broader and clearer, and at last it gets almost finished in my head, even when it is a long piece, so that I can see the **whole** of it at a single glance in my mind, as if it were a beautiful painting or a handsome human being; in which way I do not hear it in my imagination at all as a succession – the way it must come later – but all at once as it were. It is a rare feast. All the **inventing** and **making** goes on in me as in a beautiful strong dream. But the best of all is the hearing of it all at once.*

I have put key words in bold to emphasize the close relation of the two concepts of holistic and imaginative work in this particular passage. Thinking in wholes and thinking in pictures often go together, hand in hand.

> *'The whole is more than the sum of its parts.'*

Idea 40: Leaders need imagination

People have to use imagination where the need for real creation arises, where past experience gives only the slightest clue or guide, where, clearly, a novel line must be taken.

Ordway Tead, US educator

When asked to rate the attributes that contributed to their success, a selection of the world's top chief executives put *Imagination* in the fifth position out of 25 qualities. It came hard on the heels of *Ability to make decisions*, *Leadership*, *Integrity* and *Enthusiasm*. Would you put it that high on your list?

Your imagination can be developed with a little thought and effort. It is your ability to picture a new combination of ideas in a meaningful and useful relation.

The ability to imagine, the ability to create in advance in one's own mind, can be used to devise a new plan or line of action, for example. The test will be that when it is tried out it will prove to be practical and profitable.

Imagination works more freely than reasoning in that the results it seeks are not quite so specific nor so obviously explicit in the given facts. It is seeking a relationship that can be rationally established tomorrow, rather than one that is there already today.

Invention, as you know, is the use of imagination in order to solve a special kind of problem. But you can be equally inventive in the field of, say, corporate structure or team building or human relations as is the inventor in his or her workshop. Your workshop is the world of people at work.

> Can I recall one of my own problems where good results were obtained by thinking about it imaginatively?

Idea 41: Imaginative thinking

As a rule, indeed, grown-up people are fairly correct on matters of fact; it is in the higher gift of imagination that they are so sadly to seek.

Kenneth Grahame, author of *The Wind in the Willows*

Our minds have a fundamental visual capacity: we not only see things but we can shut our eyes and remember the picture of what we have seen.

It is useful to bear in mind the pictorial dimension of imagination but, beyond a certain point, it is better to use the word in a much broader sense. Avoid getting too hooked on trying to see or make mental pictures – you can think imaginatively without them. Equally, you can imagine pictures without thinking. A worried person, for example, tends to picture all sorts of imaginary scenarios in their mind; they may be feeling anxious but they are certainly not *thinking*.

In other situations we are inclined to distinguish imagining and thinking as merely being different. For example, if you are planning a holiday in Peru, you might read some books that start you thinking analytically about the climate, flora and fauna, while at the same time you may be trying to visualize what the country looks like and what the people there are like. You will be thinking, as it were, both like a physical geographer and also like an artist.

But there is a group of situations in which a person's thinking and imagination are really inseparable, and thinking is truly imaginative. Take a good detective or a top-class scientist. In trying to work out problems, they need to be both fertile in imagining feasible hypotheses and also careful about their data and what can be properly deduced. They must think imaginatively, but also in a coherent, methodical and unfanciful way.

We find it hard to rid ourselves of the assumption that imagination is exercised only in dreaming up fictional things or happenings. William Shakespeare invented living worlds of fictional characters and incidents. But Leonardo da Vinci and Thomas Edison had good imaginations too. Prospero and Hamlet are imaginary people, but the submarine and helicopter, the electric light bulb and the telephone are not imaginary objects, though it needed a combination of imagination and technical knowledge to invent them. Do you see what I mean?

Successful chief executives rate such integrated thinking and imagination high on the list of attributes they value most (see Idea 40). How does it contribute to business success? Here is Lord Sainsbury's evaluation:

> *The characteristic in a good manager which I appreciate almost above all else is that of the imagination. The good manager has to be imaginative in order to be a successful innovator. Success in that respect brings not only a valuable contribution to any enterprise, but also the considerable personal satisfaction of creative achievement.*
>
> *It is imagination that is needed to anticipate events and to respond to change. It is only those with a lively imagination who can really develop sensitive understanding of others, be they customers, colleagues or shop floor workers. To be able to do that is a vital ingredient of success in commerce or industry.*

Idea 42: Imaginative abilities of the mind

Imagination is more important than knowledge. For while knowledge defines all we currently know and understand, imagination points to all we might yet discover and create.

Albert Einstein, German physicist

The human mind has a remarkable range of imaginative abilities, from memory function at one end of the scale to creative imagination at the other.

◆ *Recalling* – The ability to bring a picture back to mind, something not actually present to the senses, such as your house or car.

◆ *Visualizing* – The ability to form a picture of something not experienced in its entirety, such as what it would be like for you to walk on the moon.

◆ *Creating* – The ability to form an image or whole of something actually nonexistent at present, such as a new product.

◆ *Foreseeing* – The ability to see a development or outcome before it materializes.

◆ *Fantasy* – The ability to invent the novel and the unreal by altering or combining the elements of reality in a particularly unrestrained and extravagant way.

 Does my imagination have real thrust and life? Can it get me off the runways of perceived reality?

Idea 43: Exercise your imagination

You can't depend on your eyes when your imagination is out of focus.

Mark Twain, author of *Adventures of Huckleberry Finn*

Just take a moment and think of the house or flat you live in. Now think of your car. When you've done that, notice that what happened is that two pictures involuntarily came into your mind. You can't help it, it's your imagination at work.

Exercise 1

Imagine you are climbing Everest by yourself and without oxygen. You are 1,000 metres from the summit.

◆ Sit down and make a meal for yourself. Work through each of your five senses to complete the scene in your mind.

◆ You are now pressing on to the summit. What can you see? What are you touching? What are your feelings? What colours can you see?

◆ Now imagine that you are on the summit. You have a camera with you. Set it up on a rock. Stand back. Now compose in detail the photograph you have taken. Turn it into a three-dimensional picture.

Exercise 2

Imagine for a moment that an unknown animal had been discovered deep in the jungles of South America. It is destined to replace the dog and the cat in popularity as a domestic pet during this century. What does it look like? What are its winning characteristics? Take some paper now and draw it, making some notes about your sketch.

In Exercise 1 you are trying to imagine a scene that really exists – you will have seen photographs or film of the summit of Everest even though you may not have been there yourself.

In Exercise 2, however, you are using your imagination to create something that doesn't exist.

I have now had a look at your picture. Well done! You certainly have a vivid imagination.

Your new animal seems to have short, silky fur like a mole. Its face looks as if it may have been borrowed from a koala bear and its round cuddly body from a wombat.

I notice that it is blue in colour and green in temperament, for it does not foul the pavements or parks. Did you borrow that from the cat family? It repels unwanted intruders more effectively than a guard dog, but is as gentle with children as a white rabbit. Wow! Where can I order one?

What you are tending to do, consciously or subconsciously, is to borrow characteristics from the animals you know. There is nothing wrong with that. Humans cannot make anything out of nothing.

You should find great encouragement in these words. You don't have to be creative in the sense of making something out of nothing – that prerogative belongs to God. Human creativity is of the second order. The potential materials – the elements, constituents or substances of which something can be made or composed – are all here in our universe. Our creative task is to combine them together in new and useful ways.

Deposits of the ores of copper and tin are very seldom found close together in nature. It was man who located them, brought them together and combined them to make bronze – the first great creative leap forward in the history of civilization.

Notice, however, that we tend to bestow the word 'creative' on products that are very far removed from the original raw materials that were used.

A masterpiece by Rubens, for example, was once a collection of blue, red, yellow and green worms of paint on the artist's palette. Now the physical materials – paints and canvas for an artist, paper and pen for an author – are entirely secondary.

Creation here is much more about what happens in the mind. Perception, ideas and feelings are combined in a concept or vision. Of course, the artist, writer or composer needs skill and technique to form on canvas or paper what is conceived in the mind.

The same principle holds good for creativity in general. Our creative imagination must have something to work on. We do not form new ideas out of nothing. But it is in the crucible of imagination that the really new and innovative is given birth.

> *'When it comes to developing your imagination, remember the principle: Use it or lost it.'*

> Creativity is the faculty of mind, hand and spirit that enables us to bring something new into existence from the available elements, something of use, order, beauty or significance.

You will be more creative when you start seeing or making connections between ideas that appear to others to be far apart: the wider the apparent distance, the greater the degree of creative thinking involved. Others will be the judge of the value you create.

Idea 44: Imagination in action

Vision is the art of seeing things invisible.

Jonathan Swift

Imaginative thinking is not limited to inventing things. The detective or the manager are usually not inventing or making anything, but they are still thinking imaginatively. They are also linked in that they both have an adversary – the criminal in one case and competitors in another. Sports people and soldiers share that factor as well.

Again, let's look at an example. When a famous football player is being praised for playing imaginatively, he is not being fêted for fantasizing in his armchair or writing novels about football. Rather, he is seen to do things such as the following:

◆ In trying to get past the opposing player he doesn't use the same jink or swerve time after time – or he may do so three times, just in order to surprise his opponent on the fourth occasion with a different change of direction.

◆ He doesn't assume that his team mate will pass out to the right, as he did the last five times – he is ready for the ball to come to him this time.

◆ He quickly realizes a gap is likely to open up where, at the moment, no gap can be seen.

In other words, he is quick to anticipate, to see and act on things that are out of the ordinary. He surprises his opponents and yet is not taken by surprise. He exploits the unexpected and the lack of routine.

This imaginative thinking on the football field has nothing to do with whether or not the player concerned writes fictional stories about football. It also has nothing to do with the rational and logical thinking prized so highly by the academics. Ron Greenwood, a former manager of the England football team, once said that 'football is a battle of wits' for which a combination of physical and mental attributes is needed:

> *A football brain is quite different from an academic brain. I coached at Oxford University for seven years and if the students had had the right kinds of football brains they would have been the best team in the world. But they didn't and they weren't. A man who can hardly read or write can have a great football brain.*

Successful generals down the ages have shown the same capacity. Winston Churchill once wrote:

> *Nearly all the battles which are regarded as the masterpieces of the military art have been battles of manoeuvre in which very often the enemy has found himself defeated by some novel device, some unexpected thrust or strategy. In such battles the losses of the victor have been small and the enemy is left puzzled as well as beaten.*

In business your next move is not blueprinted for you. It's true that you don't have total freedom. You don't have the freedom of, say, someone writing a television script or the composer of a poem. But you are like a person crossing an unmapped plateau.

You have to think up for yourself and then experimentally try out possible ways of getting where you want to be – and the solutions to these problems are not in books, nor can they be recalled from your memory bank. For you have never been here before. You have to originate or innovate, and you cannot innovate by following established precedents or by applying common recipes. That is why imagination is so important for you as a leader and manager.

> ⚠ It is imagination that is needed to anticipate events and to respond to change.

Idea 45: Imagination in perspective

Integrity without knowledge is weak and useless, and knowledge without integrity is dangerous and dreadful.

Samuel Johnson, English lexicographer

Imagination should not be promoted to top place in the hierarchy of thinking abilities. It should be a team player, not the captain. It is the vanguard, the advance scouting party of thinking. The specific role of imagination is to lead us into *innovating*, *inventing*, *creating*, *exploring*, *risk-taking* and *adventuring*.

The leader who knowingly ventures off or beyond the beaten track, the path of well-trodden expectations, is showing some degree of imagination. His or her business ventures may turn out to be fruitless, random or crazy.

For leaders who dream, dreams may be pathfinders, but they may also lead to the bankruptcy courts. Of those who depart from well-established ways only a few are explorers. *Imaginative*, *inventive* and *adventurous* are terms of praise, but equally *fanciful*, *reckless* and *crazy* describe those who are failed imaginative thinkers. Go to the history of banking in this century for your own case studies!

Be on guard, therefore, against any tendency to glorify the notion of imagination as an end in itself. People sometimes forget that a lively imagination can also be a silly one. Scope for originality is also freedom to be a crackpot. Both the genius and the crank are imaginative thinkers – some are both at the same time.

Yet imagination covers some crucial qualities in the business leader. There will be plenty of situations in your future career that will call on your powers of originating, inventing, improvising, discovering, innovating, exploring, experimenting and knowingly leaving the beaten track. Can you now see yourself doing all those things with confidence and good judgement?

Using your imagination

- ◆ Do you see yourself as having an analytical mind that is sometimes imaginative, or an imaginative mind that is also analytical?
- ◆ When you visualize yourself, the concept you have of yourself, do you see or sense considerable potential waiting to be realized inside you?
- ◆ Imagine yourself in five years' time as a chief executive with a proven reputation for imaginative action. How did you acquire that reputation? Create three more or less credible fantasies to explain your sudden emergence from the pack.

Idea 46: Quantity or quality?

New ideas are essential for industry, commerce and the public sector. New products and new ways of doing things are the lifeblood of successful enterprise.

We all have new ideas. We vary, however, in terms of the *quantity* we produce in our lifetime, and still more in the *quality* of those ideas. People who have many new ideas *with a high rate of excellent ones* among them are the ones we tend to call creative thinkers.

High	A	C
	High productivity and few quality ideas	Many quality ideas in high quality
	B	D
	Not very productive and not producing many 'pearls'	Many quality ideas with low productivity
Low	QUALITY OF IDEAS	High

PRODUCTIVITY OF IDEAS

Creativity ratios

Case study: R Buckminster Fuller

An example of an A-type thinker is Dr R Buckminster Fuller, an inventor, engineer, architect-designer and philosopher. After being expelled from Harvard and failing as a businessman, he turned to architecture and invention.

One of the most controversial architectural figures of our time, he produced designs for unprecedented types of structure that reflected his belief and optimism in the benefits of modern technology. Thus his Dymaxion House of 1927 saw the modern home not in terms of a walled structure but as technology servicing the human life within it. The house hung from a mast on a wire construction. The Dymaxion three-wheeled car of 1932 similarly rejected the traditional coachmaker's craft to produce a futuristic design.

But none of Fuller's inventions caught on before he conceived the Geodesic Dome, a linking of triangles into a strong and lightweight sphere. It was another result of his relentless pursuit of architectural forms along the path of mathematical logic. Architects hailed it as a genuine advance and Fuller's public image as a lovable crackpot began to change. Unlike classic domes, Fuller's did not depend on heavy vaults or flying buttresses for support. The weight load was transmitted throughout the structure, producing a high strength-to-weight ratio. More than 3,000,000 domes have since been built.

The word *creative* should be bestowed with care, otherwise by inappropriate overuse it will lose its meaning and become like salt without its flavour. Remember that when we call someone or something creative it always implies a value judgement. A good idea, for example, is commonly one that a critical mass of people find to be useful or helpful.

Therefore we should separate in our minds the two dimensions of creativity: quantity and quality. There are prolific novelists in most countries, but we can all probably think of a writer who produced only a few works of real genius. Barbara Cartland wrote over 500 romantic novels and Jane Austen just six, but whose name will live on for longer?

Idea 47: Case study – Thomas Edison

A successful man is a friend to failure.

Chinese proverb

Continually termed as being a genius, Thomas Edison gave some thought to what that meant, coming up with his famous definition: 'Genius is 1 per cent inspiration and 99 per cent perspiration.' He enlarged on this to his secretary: 'Well, about 99 per cent of it is knowledge of the things that will not work. The other 1 per cent may be genius, but the only way that I know to accomplish anything is everlastingly to keep working with patient observation.'

Even with Edison's phenomenal work rate, however, it is unlikely that most of us would come up with even one invention of the calibre of the light-bulb in the course of a lifetime. And he invented not only that but the phonograph, the telephone (concurrently in competition with Bell), the means of distributing electrical power, X-ray plates, and so on and on until the very end of his life.

The capacity of the man is almost unimaginable. He was able to conceive of machines for recording what we hear, which turned out to be the phonograph; and for recording what we see, which became the movie camera. These were outside the realm of anything existing then, so that their conceptualization was a supreme work of imagination.

Confronted with a problem, Edison was able to see how the solution might be arrived at. He could imagine, in the broadest terms, the short- and long-term consequences of his inventions. And all that lay between him and these goals was a great deal of hard work, which he could not wait to dispose of as soon as possible.

Edison's life was ruled by the excitement of the hunt. He once said to a colleague: 'Beach, I don't think Nature would be so unkind as to withhold the secret of a good storage battery if a real earnest hunt for it is made. I'm going to hunt.' And hunt he did, whether for the secret of the battery, the right filament for the incandescent bulb, the best mixture for insulating cables, or whatever the current problem might be, in the most methodical and exhaustive manner.

There was never any time to spare; as soon as one problem was disposed of, another idea was waiting to be put to the test. There was never enough time to investigate all his ideas, and he knew that.

For example, it was not in the end Edison but the Wright brothers who made a successful aeroplane, although as early as 1889 Edison told a journalist:

> *You can make up your mind . . . that these fellows who are fooling around with gasbags are wasting their time. The thing can't be done on those lines. You've got to have a machine heavier than air and then find something to lift it with. That's the trouble, though, to find the 'something'. I may find it one of these days.*

 What are the three key lessons about being an effective creative thinker that I can learn from Edison's productive life?

Follow-up test

Opening your mind

- [ ] 'People who can't make decisions quickly annoy me.' Do you agree with this statement?
- [ ] Can you list three possible side effects of living in a stage of uncertainty over a problem or decision?
    1
    2
    3
- [ ] 'Sometimes a good idea is the enemy of the best idea.' Do you agree?
- [ ] Are you able to stop worrying about intractable problems and turn them over to your depth mind – with a deadline?
- [ ] Are you consciously trying to develop your patience and perseverance as a thinker?
- [ ] While in the state of half-knowledge, uncertainty or doubt, are you continually on the look-out for possible connections 'beyond the Nine Dots'?
- [ ] Have you made a practice of always testing assumptions in order to eliminate the false ones?
- [ ] Are you fully aware of the effect that negative criticism can have on half-formed ideas?
- [ ] Is your depth mind creative in the way it fuses together things that are apparently completely separate?
- [ ] Can you recognize instances when the creative thinking process has worked for you?

Thinking outside the box

- ☐ Are you aware that you may have a set of unconscious assumptions that could be barriers to creative thinking?
- ☐ Do you sometimes consciously use your imagination when considering options in any given decision-making situation?
- ☐ 'The most original person is the one who borrows from the most sources.' Can you develop new ideas on a wide range of sources?
- ☐ Can you recall visually with great accuracy? Imagine your last holiday and see how much detail you can see in the mental pictures.
- ☐ Would you describe yourself as good at visualizing things you haven't directly experienced yourself? Could you, for example, accurately imagine what it would be like to be a member of the opposite sex? Or the president or prime minister of your country?
- ☐ Has anyone commended you for your imagination within the last year?
- ☐ Have you invented or made anything recently, at work or in your leisure time, that definitely required imagination?
- ☐ What is your plan for exercising your creative imagination in the coming year?

PART THREE

How to Be More Creative

If you know the nature of water, it is easier to row a boat.

Chinese proverb

The world does have a body of knowledge about creative thinking, how the human mind operates when it is about its business of generating new valuable ideas, which was covered in Parts One and Two.

The focus of Part Three is on the more applied area of creative thinking skills, together with some practical suggestions on how you can develop them.

Geniuses, of course, do all these things spontaneously and unself-consciously. It is second nature for them to listen to their depth mind and to feed it through observation, conversation and reading. 'There is in genius itself,' wrote Samuel Taylor Coleridge, 'an unconscious activity; indeed, that is the genius in the man of genius.'

In Part Three I shall share with you some key principles drawn from the lives of the master creators. Then the creative spirit within you will have practical guidance on how to go about its work – your contribution to the world's business.

Seventeen Greatest Ideas for Creative Thinking Skills

Idea 48: Four phases of the creative thinking process

The intellect has little to do on the road to discovery. There comes a leap in consciousness, call it intuition or what you will, and the solution comes to you and you don't know how or why.

Albert Einstein, German physicist

1 Preparation

The hard work. You have to collect and sort the relevant information, analyze the problem as thoroughly as you can, and explore possible solutions.

2 Incubation

This is the depth mind phase. Mental work – analyzing, synthesizing and valuing – continues on the problem in your subconscious mind. The parts of the problem separate and new combinations occur. These may involve other ingredients stored away in your memory.

3 Insight

The Eureka moment (see Idea 49). A new idea emerges into your conscious mind, either gradually or suddenly, like a fish flashing out of the water. These moments often occur when you are not thinking about the problem but are in a relaxed frame of mind.

4 Validation

This is where your valuing faculty comes into play. A new idea, insight, intuition, hunch or solution needs to be thoroughly tested. This is especially so if it is to form the basis for action of any kind.

Although it is useful for you to have this framework in mind, remember that the actual mental process is a lot more untidy than the above framework suggests.

> Think of the phases as being four chords on a piano that can be played in different sequences according to the musical requirements of the hour.

Idea 49: The Eureka moment

Eureka (Greek *heureka*) means 'I have found it'. Today we use it as an exclamation of delight at having made a discovery. Archimedes, the Greek mathematician and inventor, originally uttered it when he discovered how to test the purity of Hiero's crown.

The story is that Hiero, the king of Syracuse, gave some gold to a smith to be made into a crown. On receiving it back he felt its weight and his suspicions were aroused. Had the smith fraudulently alloyed it with an inferior metal? But he couldn't prove anything. So he asked Archimedes to devise a test for its purity.

The philosopher did not know how to proceed. He gave it a great deal of thought, but still a solution eluded him. Then one morning he got into his bath, which was full to the brim. He noticed at once that some of the water spilled over. Immediately the principle came to him that a body as it is immersed must displace its own bulk of water.

Now silver is lighter than gold, he reasoned. Therefore a pound weight of silver is bulkier than a pound weight of gold and would consequently displace more water. Thus he found out how to work out a simple method to establish if the crown was deficient in gold! As an early writer recorded:

> *When the idea flashed upon his mind, the philosopher jumped out of the bath exclaiming 'Heureka! Heureka!' and, without waiting to dress himself, ran home to try the experiment.*

Can I identify in this story four identifiable phases of creative thinking: *preparation, incubation, insight* and *validation*? Have I ever had a similar experience? (I don't mean rushing naked through the streets!)

Idea 50: Use the stepping stones of analogy

I invent nothing; I rediscover.

Auguste Rodin, French sculptor

One characteristic of creative thinkers that you can learn from is the use they make of analogy, the resemblance in some particulars between things that are otherwise unlike. Most of us see the differences, but we miss the underlying principle and its possible transferability to other uses. Natural analogies are often rich in these hidden uses.

There are other later stages, of course, but let us stop here. The point is that the model you have reached may well have been suggested by an analogy from nature.

Indeed, you could look on nature as a storehouse of analogies just waiting to be used by inventors. Radar, for example, came from studying the uses of reflected sound waves from bats. The way a clam shell opens suggested the design for aircraft cargo doors. The built-in system weakness of the pea pod suggested a way of opening cigarette packages, a method now widely used in the packaging industry.

Exercise 1

List specific inventions that were (or might have been) suggested to creative thinkers by the following natural phenomena:

   a. human arms

   b. cats

   c. seagulls

   d. a frozen salmon

   e. spiders

f. earthworms
g. a flower
h. the eye of a fly
i. conical shells
j. animal bone structures

Exercise 2

Can you add to that list? Take a piece of paper and see if you can add at least five other inventions that have sprung into the inventor's mind by using an analogy as a stepping stone.

1.
2.
3.
4.
5.

Exercise 3

Here are some more natural phenomena that could have suggested inventions to alert creative thinkers. Can you identify what these inventions might have been?

a. dew drops on leaves
b. human skulls
c. bamboo
d. human foot
e. human lungs
f. larynx

The answers are in the Appendix.

What these exercises show is that the models for the solutions to our problems do not necessarily have to be created from nothing, because they probably already exist. The same fundamental principle can be applied to all creative thinking, not just to inventing new products.

Take human organization as an example. Most of the principles involved can be found in nature: hierarchy (baboons), division of labour (ants, bees), networks (spiders' webs) and so on.

If you are trying to create a new organization you will find plenty of ready-made models in human society, past or present. Remember, however, that these are only analogies. If you copy directly you are heading for trouble.

Unlike literature where analogies – in the form of metaphors and similes – are used for literary ornament, in creative thinking you will be using comparisons or analogies as tools of thought. They are good can-openers.

Idea 51: Case study – The Buddha's statue

Soichiro Honda was an engineer who excelled in creative thinking and innovation. Early in his career, while he was building his first four-cylinder motorcycle, he gradually realized that although the engine was fine, his designers had made the whole machine look squat and ugly.

Honda decided to take a week's break for meditation and quiet reflection in Kyoto, the old imperial capital of Japan. One day, sitting in an ancient temple, he found himself fascinated by the face of a statue of the Buddha. He felt that he could see a resemblance between the look of Buddha's face and how he imagined the front of his new motorbike should be.

Having spent the rest of the week studying other statues of the Buddha in Kyoto's temples, Honda returned refreshed and inspired to his factory. Here he worked with his team of designers to produce a truly harmonious style that reflected the beauty he had glimpsed on the statue of the Buddha's face.

You can see that thinking by analogy – or analogizing, as it is sometimes called – plays a key part in all imaginative thinking. This is especially so when it comes to creative thinking.

Nature sometimes suggests to the curious and alert mind models and principles for the solutions of problems. But there are other models or analogies to be found, for example in existing man-made products and various forms of human organization. Some simple research may save you the bother of thinking a solution out for yourself.

'Don't reinvent the wheel. See what is out there already.'

Idea 52: Make the strange familiar

The process of understanding anything or anyone unfamiliar, foreign, unnatural, unaccountable – what is not already known, heard or seen – is best begun by relating it by analogy to what we know already.

Often you cannot get where you need in one jump. But if you can hit on a good analogy, you are halfway there, like crossing a stream on stepping stones.

When, for example, indigenous inhabitants of New Guinea saw an aircraft for the first time, they called it the 'big bird'. Birds were familiar to them. Their first step towards comprehending something totally strange or unfamiliar was to assume it was an unusual example of something already known to them.

Case study: The chemistry of leadership

Not too long ago I conducted a seminar on leadership for heads of university departments. Leadership and management, and the difference between them, were quite new concepts for many of the participants. One of them, a professor of chemistry, used the familiar to understand the unfamiliar in this way. In a letter to me later he explained:

In chemistry a reaction between two compounds that can react is often put down in notation as follows:

$$A + B \rightleftarrows AB$$

Many reactions proceed slowly, if at all, without a catalyst. This to my mind is the role of leadership in getting a job done – to catalyse the process.

Notice that we tend to apply this principle of seeking to understand the strange or unfamiliar by comparing it to what is familiar in our social life. As the American novelist John Steinbeck said, 'No man really knows about other human beings. The best he can do is to suppose that they are like himself.'

Case study: My brother Jack

Two mothers are waiting outside a school to collect their children at the end of the day and chatting. 'Your Jane's new boyfriend Mark is just like my brother Jack used to be, the life and soul of the party,' said one. 'They've got the same sense of humour. Jack was a devil with the girls, too,' she continued, 'so I don't expect it will last long.'

'Didn't you tell me that Jack had a bit of a temper?' asked her companion.

'He certainly did. I have warned Jane to watch out for that, as I am sure it's there. Though, to tell you the truth, he has been as mild as a lamb – so far.'

As a form of reasoning, analogy has to be handled carefully. *All analogies break down at some point.* You need to know when to jump off the train. In the story above, for example, Mark certainly is analogous to Jack in two respects. But there are no grounds for believing that the analogy will hold in the other respects mentioned.

Idea 53: Make the familiar strange

The aspect of things that are most important for us are hidden because of their simplicity and familiarity.

Ludwig Wittgenstein, Austrian philosopher

If you see things or people repeatedly you hardly observe them at all unless there is some change from the familiar or predictable, some deviation from the norm, which forces itself on your attention. As Roman philosopher Seneca said, 'Familiarity reduces the greatness of things.'

However, seeing something as strange, odd, problematic, unsatisfactory or only half-known restarts the engines of your mind. Remember the proverb 'God hides things (and people) from us by putting them near to us.'

Exercise

Take something that you frequently see or experience, or perhaps an everyday occurrence like the sun rising or the rain falling.

Set aside half an hour with some paper and a pen or pencil. Reflect or meditate on the object, concentrating on what you *don't* know about it.

When we say we know someone we usually mean that we have a hazy notion of their likes and dislikes, together with a rough idea of their personality or temperament. We believe we can predict more or less accurately how the person will react. We think we know when our relative or friend is deviating from their normal behaviour. But take yourself as an example. Does anyone know everything about you? Could you in all honesty say that you fully know yourself?

'We do not know people – their concerns, their loves and hates, their thoughts,' said the late novelist Iris Murdoch in a television interview. 'For me the people I see around me every day are more extraordinary than any characters in my books.' The implication is that below the surface of familiarity there is a wonderful unknown world to be explored.

This morning you may have made a cup of tea or coffee and had your breakfast, the same as yesterday. But was it? You will never even brush your teeth in precisely the same way as yesterday. Every day, every hour, every minute is unique. As French author Proust reminds us: 'Be aware, always and at every moment, that the miracle is in the here and now.'

> *'Discovery consists of seeing what everyone has seen and thinking what nobody has thought.'*

Idea 54: Widen your span of relevance

It is the function of creative people to perceive the relations between thoughts, or things or forms of expression that may seem utterly different, and to combine them into some new forms – the power to connect the seemingly unconnected.

William Plomer, South African author

Farming in his native Berkshire in the early eighteenth century, the British agriculturalist Jethro Tull developed a drill enabling seeds to be sown mechanically, and so spaced that cultivation between rows was possible in the growth period.

Tull was an organist, and it was the principle of the organ that gave him his new idea. What he was doing, in effect, was to transfer the technical means of achieving a practical purpose from one field to another.

The essential ingredients of the story are as follows. Tull was confronted with a problem and dissatisfied with the existing solutions to it. Suddenly a spark jumped between the problem and his knowledge of another technology. He found a model or analogy. Then it was a question of applying the principle and developing the technology for the new task in hand. The less obvious the connection between the two fields, the more we are likely to call it creative thinking.

Therefore it is not surprising that inventors and other creative thinkers have knowledge in more than one field. They may even work in a quite different sphere from the one in which they make their names as discoverers or inventors.

> **Exercise**
>
> Guess the main occupation of the inventors of the following products:
>
> | Invention | Occupation |
> | --- | --- |
> | 1 Ballpoint pen | _____ |
> | 2 Safety razor | _____ |
> | 3 Kodachrome films | _____ |
> | 4 Automatic telephone | _____ |
> | 5 Parking meter | _____ |
> | 6 Pneumatic tyre | _____ |
> | 7 Long-playing record | _____ |
>
> See the Appendix for the answers.

So the transfer of technology from one field to another, usually with some degree of alteration and adaptation, is one way in which you can make a creative contribution.

You may be familiar with a body of knowledge or technical capability unknown to others in your field because you have worked in more than one industry. Or it may come about as a result of your travels to other countries.

Sir Barnes Wallis, the British aeronautical engineer who helped to develop the Concorde supersonic airliner and the swing-wing aircraft, failed his London matriculation examination at the age of 16. 'I knew nothing,' he said in a television interview, 'except how to think, how to grapple with a problem and then go on grappling with it until you had solved it.'

When you are grappling with a problem remember to *widen your span of relevance*. Look at the technologies available in fields other than your own, possibly in those that may appear to others to be so far removed as to be irrelevant. They may give you a clue.

'Experience has shown,' wrote Edgar Allan Poe, 'that a vast, perhaps the larger, portion of the truth arises from the seemingly irrelevant.'

People with a narrow span of relevance are thinking within the tramlines and boundaries of their own industry. Leap over the wall! Develop a wide span of relevance, for there are connections between every other industry in the world and yours – if only you could see them.

It comes down to your 'power to connect the seemingly unconnected', or at least the things that hitherto have not been brought together in a new and interesting relation.

 Can I think of one instance where I have experienced 'the power to connect the seemingly unconnected'?

Idea 55: Keep your eyes open

If a man looks sharply and attentively, he shall see Fortune; for though she is blind yet she is not invisible.

Francis Bacon, English philosopher

'I am fascinated by the principle of growth: how people and things evolved,' said the portrait painter Graham Sutherland in an interview at the age of 73. He aimed to pin down the atmosphere and essence of the people he painted: 'I have to be as patient and watchful as a cat.' He could see in the human face the same sort of expression of the process of growth and struggle as he found in the rugged surfaces of boulders or the irregular contours of a range of hills. 'There are so many ideas I want to get off my chest. The days aren't long enough,' he added.

It may seem odd to think of painting a picture as a means of getting an idea off your chest. But for the artist the act of careful, analytical observation is only part of the story. Ideas and emotions are fused into the paint in the heat of inspiration. What the artist knows and feels is married to what he or she sees, and the picture is the child of that union.

'Painting is a blind man's profession,' said Picasso. 'He paints not what he sees, but what he feels, what he tells himself about what he has seen.' That principle holds true not only for the kind of art for which Picasso is famous, but also for the more realistic work of painters such as Graham Sutherland.

An observation made through the eyes will undergo transformation to varying degrees in the creative mind as it is combined with other elements into a new idea, bubbling away in a cauldron of animated interest. As William Blake put it, 'A fool sees not the same tree that a wise man sees.' But the observation itself needs to be clear, accurate and honest. Like a good cook, a creative thinker should work from the best materials.

About 70 per cent of the information we use comes through our eyes. Therefore you should develop your ability to see things and make detailed observations. For they are the materials for future creative thinking.

Case Study: Laurence Olivier

Laurence Olivier was an actor renowned for his ability to build character in a creative way. 'I am like a scavenger,' he said, 'I observe closely, storing some details for as long as 18 years in my memory.'

When invited to play the title role in Shakespeare's *King Richard the Third* he drew on his recollection of Jed Harris, a famous Broadway producer of the 1930s, under whom he had a bad experience. Harris had a prominent nose, which Olivier borrowed for the role, along with elements of his disagreeable character.

But Olivier combined other elements into the new role, such as the shadow of the Big Bad Wolf, which he had seen long ago in Walt Disney's film *Pinocchio*. Remembered films often gave him such ideas. The little dance he did while playing Shylock came from Hitler's jig for joy when France signed its capitulation in 1940, a moment shown on German newsreels.

Observation is a skill. 'You see, but you do not observe,' comments Sherlock to his assistant Dr Watson in one of their cases. At the lowest level it implies the ability to see what is really in front of you. Laurence Olivier added to that skill a retentive memory for what he had observed with interest.

Notice, too, how Olivier was able to combine elements in his memory into a coherent whole – a new stage character. What may give you this kind of inspiration?

Idea 56: Observational skills

If I ever made any valuable discoveries, it has been owing more to patient attention than to any other talent.

Isaac Newton, English scientist

One of the best forms of training in observation is drawing or sketching.

A great pioneer in the importance of teaching drawing, John Ruskin, once told his students at the Working Men's College in London in the 1850s, 'I am only trying to teach you to see.'

Seeing, for Ruskin, was the fundamental way in which to acquire knowledge of the world, and he believed it was a talent that few possessed. As he wrote in *Modern Painters*:

The greatest thing a human soul ever does in this world is to see something, and tell what it saw in a plain way. Hundreds of people can talk for one who can think, but thousands can think for one who can see. To see clearly is poetry, prophecy and religion – all in one.

Would you like to try it for yourself?

Exercise 1

Take some paper and pencil and look at any object, such as a teapot, cup and saucer or vase of flowers. Select from what you see the key lines that give you its essential shape. You are now exercising careful and analytical attention. This phase should take about five minutes.

Now draw the object as you see it. Allow no more than five minutes for this second sketching phase.

Do not worry if you cannot reproduce the object like a trained artist. Your aim is different. You are using sketching as a means of learning to use your eyes, so that you can really see the world around you.

Exercise 2

The next time you go to a railway station, make a list of five things you have never seen before.

Exercise 3

Select one area in your work responsibilities for special attention in the next week, such as the layout of goods in a shop or the pattern of customer calls. Simply observe and collect data on it, like a scientist studying the seashore or butterflies. Don't attempt to draw any conclusions, for the object of the exercise is solely to increase your powers of observation.

Observation implies attempting to see a person, object or scene as if you had never seen it before in your life. What it really teaches us is not experience, but observation.

> The ability to give careful, analytical and honest attention to what you see is essential. If you do not notice and observe, you will not think.

> ' "All our knowledge has its origins in our perceptions," wrote artist and inventor Leonardo da Vinci. Make sure that you see things clearly and accurately.'

Idea 57: Test your assumptions

Daring ideas are like chessmen moved forward. They may be beaten, but they may start a winning game.

Johann Wolfgang von Goethe, German author

Albert Einstein is famous for making one assumption and thinking out its implications. 'Let me assume,' he said to himself, 'that I am riding on the back of a sunbeam, travelling through the universe with the speed of light. How would things look to me?' The eventual result was the General Theory of Relativity!

It was by formulating this theory that Einstein led us to the knowledge that planets and stars move not because they are influenced by forces coming from other bodies in the universe, but because of the special nature of the world of space and time in the neighbourhood of matter.

Light-rays may travel straight, for example, in the vast interstellar spaces, but they are deflected or bent when they come within the field of influence of a star or other massive body.

Making *conscious* assumptions like the one that Einstein made – *as if* thinking – is a key tool in the tool chest of a creative thinker. You are *deliberately* and *temporarily* making a supposition that something is true.

It is like making a move in a game of chess but still keeping your hand on the piece, so that you can replace it if you do not like the implications of the half-made move. 'No great discovery is made without a bold guess,' said Isaac Newton.

I have emphasized the words *conscious*, *deliberately* and *temporarily* because this kind of exploratory thinking does need to be sharply distinguished from thinking based on *unconscious* assumptions or preconceptions.

We have all had the experience of taking something for granted as the basis for opinion or action, and then subsequently finding that we had made an erroneous assumption – probably an unconscious one – that was unwarranted.

Watch out for these preconceptions! They are like hidden sandbanks outside the harbour mouth. Develop your awareness of the tangled misconceptions, preconceptions and unconscious assumptions within you. Welcome others when they challenge or question your assumptions.

Think outside the box! Don't allow yourself to be constrained by the mental limitations or straitjackets that are sometimes imposed on situations without any warrant or truth.

> *'If you are not prepared to be wrong, you'll never come up with anything original.'*

Making an assumption is more like taking a tentative step. *'Supposing we did it this way – how would it work? What would the consequences be?'* It is not an answer, even a guessed answer, but it is a step that you can take if you are baffled, which might open up new possibilities.

Louis Pasteur compared assumptions to 'searchlights which illumine the path of an experimenter and serve him as a guide to interrogate nature'. He added: 'They become a danger only if he transforms them into fixed ideas.'

Remember always that suppositions are to be made without commitment, like trying on new clothes in a shop before buying (or not buying) them.

How good am I at creating in my mind these temporary or provisional stepping-stones of thought?

Idea 58: Do not wait for inspiration

Thou, O God, dost sell us all good things at the price of labour.

Leonardo da Vinci, Renaissance artist and inventor

'I can call spirits from the vastly deep,' boasts Owen Glendower in Shakespeare's *Henry IV*. Hotspur puts down the fiery Celt by replying: 'Why so can I, or so can any man, but will they come when you do call for them?' Doubtless Shakespeare is writing here from personal experience. The comings and goings of inspiration are unpredictable.

In creative work it is unwise to wait for the right mood. English author Graham Greene once said:

> *Writing has to develop its own routine. When I'm seriously at work on a book, set to work first thing in the morning, about seven or eight o'clock, before my bath or shave, before I've looked at my post or done anything else. If one had to wait for what people call 'inspiration', one would never write a word.*

Thriller writer Leslie Thomas agreed:

> *People are always asking me, 'Do you wait for inspiration?' But any novelist who does that is going to starve. I sit down, usually without an idea in my head, and stare at the proverbial blank paper; once I get going, it just goes.*

It can seem impossible, like trying to drive a car with more water in the tank than petrol. But you just have to get out and push. Better to advance by inches than not to advance at all.

As we saw in Idea 47, Thomas Edison, inventor of the electric light bulb among many other things, gave a celebrated definition of genius as '1 per cent inspiration and 99 per cent perspiration'.

Creative thinking, paradoxically, is not very creative for 99 hours out of every 100. What it is can be described as endlessly varied combinations of analyzing, synthesizing, imagining and valuing. The raw materials are sifted, judged, adapted, altered and glue together in different ways until something creative results.

When Queen Victoria congratulated the world-renowned pianist Paderewski on being a genius he replied: 'That may be, Ma'am, but before I was a genius I was a drudge.'

Not all intellectual drudges are geniuses, however. Something more is needed. That lies beyond the willingness to start work without tarrying for inspiration and to keep at it day in and day out.

Idea 59: Leave a candle in the window

Inspiration seldom hits you with the force of a sledgehammer. It is more like a butterfly that may alight within reach after you have abandoned the chase with your net. But if your eyes are shut, you won't even notice the uninvited yet beautiful guest.

We all need inspiration every day. Therefore, in order to experience it, be awake and alert, always ready for the faint stirring in the air, with the doors of your mind open and a candle in the window to guide it home.

In other words, you need a peculiar kind of sensitivity, as if you were standing still and waiting, prepared and ready with all your senses alert, for the faintest brush of the wind in the treetops.

Your inner ear or eye may trace some delicate motion in your deeper mind, some thought that stirs like a leaf in the unseen air. It is not the stillness, nor the half-thought that only stirred, but these three mysteries in one that together constitute the experience of inspiration.

German poet Goethe used a more homely image:

> *The worst is that the very hardest thinking will not bring thoughts. They must come like good children of God and cry 'Here we are'. But neither do they come unsought. You expend effort and energy thinking hard.*
>
> *Then, after you have given up, they come sauntering in with their hands in their pockets. If the effort had not been made to open the door, however, who knows if they would have come?*

We have all been given a mind capable of creative thinking and there is no going back on that. So we are more than halfway there. We just have to believe that there are words and music in the air, if we tune in our instruments to the right wavelengths. They will come in their own time and to their own place.

'Inspiration favours the ready mind.'

Idea 60: Case study – James Watt

One should never impose one's views on a problem; one should rather study it, and in time a solution will reveal itself.

Albert Einstein, German physicist

James Watt, the celebrated Scottish engineer and inventor, found that the condenser for the Newcomen steam engine, which he studied closely at the University of Glasgow, was very inefficient.

Power for each stroke was developed by first filling the cylinder with steam and then cooling it with a jet of water. This cooling action condensed the steam and formed a vacuum behind the piston, which the pressure of the atmosphere then forced to move.

Watt calculated that this process of alternately heating and cooling the cylinder wasted three-quarters of the heat supplied to the engine.

Therefore Watt realized that if he could prevent this loss, he could reduce the engine's fuel consumption by more than 50 per cent. He worked for two years on the problem with no solution in sight. Then, one fine Sunday afternoon, he was out walking:

I had entered the green and had passed the old washing house. I was thinking of the engine at the time. I had gone as far as the herd's house when the idea came into my mind that as steam was an elastic body it would rush into a vacuum, and if a connection were made between the cylinder and an exhausting vessel it would rush into it and might then be condensed without cooling the cylinder . . . I had not walked further than the Golf house when the whole thing was arranged in my mind.

Five practical lessons

1   Do not wait for inspiration or you will wait for ever. Inspiration is a companion that will appear beside you

on certain stretches of the road. 'One sits down first,' said the French dramatist, novelist and film director Jean Cocteau, 'one thinks afterwards.'

2   'The intellect has little to do on the road to discovery,' said Albert Einstein. 'There comes a leap in conscious-ness, call it intuition or what you will, and the solution comes to you and you don't know how or why.'

3   Develop an inner sensitivity or awareness, so that your spiritual eyes and ears are open to the slightest move-ment or suggestion from outside or inside, from above or below, which hints at a way forward. Listen to your inklings!

4   You cannot quite control the process that leads to genuine creative work. But having the right attitude of expectancy, together with a measure of hope and con-fidence, certainly seems to pay off.

5   'Like a long-legged fly upon the stream, her mind moves upon silence.' These evocative words of Robert Frost underline the need for silence and solitude in creative thinking, such as you find on a country walk. James Watt was walking alone when his inspired idea came to him.

Somebody once asked Anton Bruckner: 'Master, how, when, where did you think of the divine motif of your *Ninth Symphony*?'

'Well, it was like this,' Bruckner replied. 'I walked up the Kahlenberg and when it got hot and I got hungry, I sat down by a little brook and unpacked my Swiss cheese, and just as I open the greasy paper that tune pops into my head!'

Do I make sufficient time available for quiet, reflective thinking?

> *'It is no good trying to shine if you don't take time to fill your lamp.'*

The best advice is not to focus too strongly on any single aspect of a problem in the early stages. You should learn to think generally or holistically about it, like a scientist scanning a problem area for flaws. Let the problem speak to you.

'Whatever the ultimate object of his work,' wrote Hazel Rossotti in *Introducing Chemistry,* 'the experimental chemist's immediate aim is to ask suitable questions of the sensible bodies he is studying and to *let them answer for themselves*. It is the chemist's job to observe and report the answers with minimal distortion; only then can he attempt to interpret them.'

Patient analysis and restructuring of the parts, taking up different perspective points in your imagination from which to view them: all these will deepen your understanding of the problem. If you're lucky, fairly soon they will release within you, like a cash dispenser, the right solution or at least the right direction in which to advance.

> When analyzing, do not be over-hasty in defining the problem. Play with alternative formulations until one emerges that commands your support.

Idea 61: Working it out

There is an old saying 'Well begun is half done.' 'Tis a bad one.
I would use instead, 'Not begun at all till half done.'

John Keats, English poet

Don't wait until you have a fully formed idea in your mind before you start work. Creative thinking continues *after* you have begun to work.

Remember that creative thinking and creativity are not quite the same. Creative thinking leads you to the new idea; creativity includes actually bringing it into existence.

There are some cases, indeed, where an idea or concept appears initially in its finished and fully fledged form, but they are the exceptions. What you are given is usually far less than that. You have to work it out.

In the process of working it out the idea may be developed, adapted or changed, and new ideas or materials will be added to the melting pot. Products and services are made in the making.

This approach rather goes against the grain for those who have been indoctrinated to seek finished ideas before going to work. But it adds greatly to the interest and excitement of work if you do not know what is coming next. 'I have never started a poem yet whose end I knew,' said Robert Frost. Creative thinking has to be an adventure.

Knowing when to stop thinking and start trying to work out an idea is an important act of judgement. If you are premature, you will waste a lot of time fruitlessly chasing ideas that are not right. But if you have a working clue, don't wait too long!

Case study: John Hunter

John Hunter, an eighteenth-century British surgeon and physiologist, had considerable influence as a teacher. His most brilliant pupil was Edward Jenner, who had already begun to think that he could prevent smallpox by vaccination with cowpox, based on the observation that milkmaids did not get smallpox.

'*Don't think,*' Hunter advised. '*Try it!* Be patient, be accurate!' And the pupil spent many years in painstaking observation. In due course, as we all know, Jenner developed a method of vaccination against smallpox that was successful in producing immunity.

Working it out – actually trying to make or produce something – is a way of continuing the process of creative thinking. Therefore it is not necessary to have a fully formed picture or crystal clear idea of where you are going before you start work.

Because so little is given to you by way of initial inspiration, you may follow false trails, get lost and feel frustrated, even to the point of despairing. But if you haven't worked on the edge of failure you haven't worked on the edge of real success.

As implementation is part of creative thinking you have to develop the product yourself, at least up to a certain point. Beyond that point it obviously has to be much more of a team effort, especially if you wish to take the idea into the marketplace.

Remember that exhilaration is that feeing you get after a great idea hits you, and just before you realize what's wrong with it!

'*Solvitur ambulando (literally, solve it as you are walking). Get moving and solutions will come to you by the wayside.*'

Idea 62: Drift, wait and obey

When your creative spirit is in charge, do not try to think consciously. Drift, wait and obey.

Rudyard Kipling, author of *The Jungle Book*

Although creative thinking requires sustained attention, sometimes over a period of years, it does not always have to be conscious attention. Indeed, it often seems that the longer you are consciously wrestling with a difficulty or problem, the less likely you are to solve it.

Try switching off your attention – 'drift, wait and obey' on the tide of thought. Wait for your unconscious mind to whisper to you: 'Hey, have you thought of this?'

What your depth mind can do for you is to connect things in unexpected or unusual ways. For Leonardo da Vinci, for example, the worlds of science and art were deeply interconnected. His notebooks were filled with pictures, colours and images; his sketchbooks for paintings abounded with geometry, anatomy and perspective. He wrote:

To develop a complete mind: Study the science of art, study the art of science. Learn how to see. Realize that everything connects to everything else.

Not a bad prospectus for a creative thinker!

Case study: The depth mind at work

In his autobiography *Long Before Forty* (1967), C S Forester, author of the Hornblower books, wrote one of the best introspective descriptions of what he sensed was going on in his depth mind:

There are jellyfish that drift about in the ocean. They do nothing to seek out their daily food; chance carries them hither and thither, and chance brings them nourishment. Small living things come into contact with their tentacles, and are seized, devoured and digested . . .

Think of me as the jellyfish, and the captured victims become the plots, the stories, the outlines, the motifs – use whatever term you may consider best to describe the framework of a novel . . .

We can go on with the analogy; once the captured victim is inside the jellyfish's stomach the digestive juices start pouring out and the material is transformed into a different protoplasm, without the jellyfish consciously doing anything about it . . .

Some morning when I am shaving, some evening when I am wondering whether my dinner calls for white wine or red, the original immature idea reappears in my mind, and it has grown . . .

Composer Tchaikovsky wrote this description of his depth mind at work:

Sometimes I observe with curiosity that uninterrupted activity, which – independent of the subject of any conversation I may be carrying on – continues its course in that department of my brain which is devoted to music. Sometimes it takes a preparatory form – that is, the consideration of all details that concern the elaboration of some projected work; another time it may be an entirely new and independent musical idea.

Obviously some vocations – inventors, playwrights, scientists and composers, for example – call for more depth mind activity than others. But the ability to make such connections, to grow new ideas or wholes, is present in all of us in varying degrees.

Remember that creativity doesn't require superhuman powers or extra-sensory perception. What happens is that your depth mind is at work, interpreting natural signs, picking up hints that invade your senses below the conscious threshold, and piecing together the paucity of information in the shape of guesses, hints or clues.

The first step is to understand that your mind *does* have this creative dimension. With a degree of simple awareness, understanding and skill, you can work with its holistic capability of growing ideas as if they were seeds connecting or integrating apparently unrelated materials, creating order out of chaos.

Skill? Yes, because there is an art in knowing when to stand back and let your depth mind do its work.

Idea 63: Sleep on the problem

Another gem from Leonardo da Vinci: 'It is no small benefit on finding oneself in bed in the dark to go over again in the imagination the main lines of the forms previously studied, or other noteworthy things conceived by ingenious speculation.' The reason, of course, is that your depth mind may then get to work while you are asleep.

Of course, you might actually dream of a solution. Dreams are extraordinary creations of our imagining faculty in the inner brain. They also give us clues to how the depth mind works, not least in the language of visual imagery.

The man who invented the Singer sewing machine, for example, reached an impasse when he could not get the thread to run through the needle consistently. When he was at his wit's end he dreamed one night that he was being chased by natives carrying spears. As they came closer, he noticed that every spear had a hole at the bottom of the blade. The next morning, he made a needle with its eye near the point, instead of at the top. His machine was complete.

> **?** Can I recall any dream which I felt communicated to me something important, relevant or interesting?

Quite why sleep plays such an important part in helping or enabling the depth mind to analyze, synthesize and value is still a mystery. Dreams suggest an inner freedom to make all sorts of random connections between different constellations of brain cells. There may be some sort of shaking up of the kaleidoscope, resulting in new patterns forming in the mine shafts of the mind. We just do not know.

This ignorance of *how* the depth mind works does not matter very much. What does matter is that it does work.

> 'It does not make any difference if the cat is black or white as long as it catches mice.'
>
> Chinese proverb

There is an element of mystery about the creative work that can go on in our sleep. Author Robert Louis Stevenson spoke of 'those little people, my brownies, who do one half my work for me while I am fast asleep, and in all human likelihood do the rest for me as well, when I am wide awake and fondly suppose I do it for myself'.

'When I am completely myself,' wrote composer Mozart to his father, 'entirely alone or during the night when I cannot sleep, it is on these occasions that my ideas flow best and most abundantly. Whence and how these come I know not nor can I force them. Nor do I hear in my imagination the parts successfully, but I hear them at the same time altogether.'

You most probably have experienced the beneficial effects of sleeping on a problem, and awakening to find that your mind has made itself up. Use that principle by programming your depth mind for a few minutes as you lie in the dark and before you go to sleep.

Your dreams may occasionally be directly relevant. It is much more likely, however, that some indication, clue or idea will occur to you after 'sleeping on it'. Perhaps during your waking hours, for instance while you are shaving or washing the dishes, the idea will dart into your mind.

Do you remember Francis Bacon's advice from Idea 30? 'A man would do well to carry a pencil in his pocket and write down the thoughts of the moment. Those that come unsought are commonly the most valuable and should be secured, because they seldom return.' To follow Bacon's wise words, always keep a pad and pencil by your bedside: when a brief idea comes, write it down.

Idea 64: Think creatively about your life

Creativeness and a creative attitude to life as a whole is not man's right, it is his duty.

Nikolai Berdyaev, Russian religious philosopher

You may not be an author of books, but you are writing the book of your own life. Your life is not being dictated to you from a pre-recorded script. You can make at least some of it up as you go along. 'When the creative urge seizes one – at least, such is my experience – one becomes creative in all directions at once,' said novelist Henry Miller.

If you decide to take a creative approach to life it does change your perspective. You will seek out first some 'given' ideas about yourself. What are your distinctive strengths? These are not easy questions to answer. Self-discovery lasts a lifetime, and even then it may not be completed. Seek to identify what you are born to excel at, and make sure you are working in the right area.

Even when some conscious self-analysis and some imaginative thinking, supplemented by intuition, have given you some clues, insights or bold guesses about yourself, you still have to try to work out these ideas in real life. That involves an element of trial and error, periods of frustration and despair, and moments of excitement and joy.

For gradually, the creative pattern of your life begins to emerge before your eyes on the loom of experience, with change and continuity as its warp and weft.

Life is a usually interesting, occasionally exciting and sometimes painful journey forwards into an unknown future. As you try to make something of it in a creative way, working things out as you go along, new ideas will come to you. Even in the desert stretches there are wells and springs of inspiration, but they are not to be had in advance.

'Twenty years from now you will be more disappointed by the things that you didn't do than by the ones you did do,' wrote Mark Twain. 'So throw off the bowlines. Sail away from the safe harbour. Catch the trade wind in your sails. Explore. Dream. Discover.'

> *'Life is an adventure.'*

Follow-up test

Creative thinking skills

- [ ] Do you have a friendly and positive attitude to your depth mind? Do you expect it to work for you?
- [ ] Where possible, do you build into your plans time to 'sleep on it', so as to give your depth mind an opportunity to contribute?
- [ ] Name one idea or intuition that has come to you unexpectedly in the last two weeks.
- [ ] What physical activities – such as walking or gardening or driving a car – do you find especially conducive to receiving the results of depth mind thinking?
- [ ] Have you experienced waking up next morning and finding that your unconscious mind has resolved some problem or made some decision for you?
- [ ] Do you see your depth mind as being like a computer? Remember the computing acronym GIGO – Garbage In, Garbage Out.
- [ ] 'Few people think more than two or three times a year,' said Irish playwright George Bernard Shaw. 'I have made an international reputation for myself by thinking once or twice a week.' How often do you deliberately seek to employ your depth mind to help you to analyze a complex matter, synthesize or restructure materials, or reach value judgements?
- [ ] How could knowledge of how the depth mind works help you in your relations with other people?

☐ What other clues have you learnt from experience – clues not indicated in this book – on how to get the best out of your unconscious mind?

☐ Can you identify and list on paper three ways in which you can improve your curiosity?

1

2

3

☐ In the next three months you will most probably sit next to a total stranger at a meal. What five questions will you ask them?

1

2

3

4

5

☐ Can you think of a manager who is more observant than you are? What beneficial results have stemmed from his/her observations?

☐ Has anyone described you as a good listener within the last 12 months?

☐ Are you an active listener, using questions like tools to prize pearls out of reluctant shells?

☐ Does reading books or articles play an important part in keeping your mind stimulated and in shape?

☐ Do you read fiction to develop and extend your imagination?

☐ Have you ever travelled in search of ideas on how to do your job better?

☐ Do you choose holidays in places that stimulate and refresh your mind as well as your body?

PART FOUR

Creative Leadership

Innovation is the key to winning – and keeping – leadership in world markets. New ideas and new ways of doing things are the main ingredients in sustained business success. But how is the necessary innovation going to be achieved? By whom? That is the theme of this book.

Innovation calls for a special form of creativity, which I call *team creativity*. Of course, all organizations are teams, or at least they are potentially so. The effective production and marketing of goods or services these days – delivery on time, at the required quality and at a competitive price – call for high-performance teamwork. But to improve those existing products and to develop new products and services requires a different order of teamwork – team creativity.

To achieve team creativity you need to be a creative leader, one who is able to manage and lead creative individuals – not sometimes the easiest of people to control – and creative groups. Part Four offers you plenty of ideas about how to develop your leadership in that direction.

If you introduce the team creativity approach into your workplace it will greatly enhance everyone's enjoyment of work. For people get much more out of work if they put their minds fully into it. As playwright Noël Coward said, 'Work is more fun than fun.'

Nine Greatest Ideas for Your Role as Creative Leader

Idea 65: Your basic role as team leader

Grace does not destroy nature but perfects it.

Thomas Aquinas, Italian philosopher,
theologian and Dominican friar

Creative leadership is not a different form of leadership to, say, effective leadership. There is a natural or generic role of leader, and you need to master that. Being or becoming a creative leader is a grace that completes or perfects your leadership contribution. Good natural leaders are taking the first steps in that direction when they share decisions with their team members.

A key issue in leadership is always how far the team leader (appointed or elected) should share decisions with others, team members or colleagues, and, beyond that, involve them fully in creative and innovative thinking. Of course, it is also an issue for all of us how far we should make our decisions after solitary and silent thought, or how far we should consult others. Should we try to generate ideas on our own or engage our team in the process?

Before looking together at the more creative aspects of leadership, the realm of great leadership, let me put it in context by reminding you of what the world knows already about the generic role of leader – the role true for all fields of work and all levels of leadership. Discovering that role in the 1960s was the greatest breakthrough in this field in my lifetime.

If you look closely at matters involving leadership, there are always three elements or variables:

1   The leader – qualities of personality and character.
2   The situation – partly constant, partly varying.
3   The group – the followers, their needs and values.

In fact, work groups are always different, just as individuals are. After coming together they soon develop a *group personality*. So that which works in one group may not work in another. All groups and organizations are unique.

But that is only half the truth. The other half is that work groups, like individuals, have certain needs in common. There are three areas of overlapping need which are centrally important, as illustrated in the diagram.

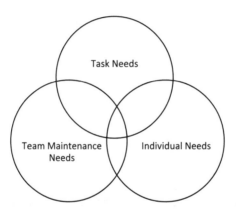

The model is a simple one. It is no longer a hypothesis or even a theory: we now know that it is true. It is simple but not simplistic or superficial. It has the quality mathematicians call *deep*. You can go on thinking about the model for the rest of your life and you will never exhaust its possibilities.

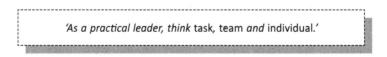

'As a practical leader, think task, team *and* individual.'

Idea 66: Task, team and individual

When people are of one mind and heart they can move Mount Tai.

> Chinese proverb (Mount Tai is a famous mountain in Shandong Province, the highest known to Confucius)

Task need

Work groups and organizations come into being because there is a task to be done that is too big for one person. You can climb a hill or a small mountain by yourself, but you cannot climb Mount Everest on your own – you need a team for that.

Why call it a need? Because pressure builds up a head of steam to accomplish the common task. People can feel very frustrated if they are prevented from doing so.

Team maintenance need

This is not as easy to perceive as the task need; as with an iceberg, much of the life of any group lies below the surface. The distinction that the task need concerns things and the team maintenance need involves people does not help much.

Again, it is best to think of groups as threatened from without by forces aimed at their disintegration or from within by disruptive people or ideas. We can then see how they give priority to maintaining themselves against these external or internal pressures, sometimes showing great ingenuity in the process.

Many of the written or unwritten rules of the group are designed to promote this unity and to maintain cohesiveness at all costs. Those who rock the boat, or infringe group standards and corporate balance, may expect reactions varying from friendly indulgence to downright anger. Instinctively a common feeling exists that 'united we stand, divided we fall'; that good relationships, desirable in themselves, are also essential means towards the shared end. This need to create and promote group cohesiveness I have called the team maintenance need.

Individual needs

Third, individuals bring into the group their own needs – not just the physical ones for food and shelter (which are largely catered for by the payment of wages these days) but also the psychological needs: recognition; a sense of doing something worthwhile; status; and the deeper needs to give to and receive from other people in a working situation. These individual needs are perhaps more profound than we sometimes realize.

They spring from the depths of our common life as human beings. They may attract us to, or repel us from, any given group. Underlying them all is the fact that people need one another not only to survive but to achieve and develop personality.

Can I identify the presence of these three kinds of need in my own environment?
What – if any – are the tensions between them?

Idea 67: The three circles interact

We cannot live only for ourselves. A thousand fibres connect us with our fellow men; and among those fibres, as sympathetic threads, our actions come as causes, and they come back to us as effects.

Herman Melville, American novelist

The three areas of need present in all working groups – task, team and individual – overlap and influence one another for good or ill.

If the common task is achieved, for example, then that tends to build the team and to satisfy personal human needs in individuals. If there is a lack of cohesiveness in the team circle, a failure of team mainte-nance, then clearly performance in the task area will be impaired and the satisfaction of individual members reduced. Thus, as shown in Idea 65, we can visualize the needs present in work groups as three overlapping and interactive circles.

Nowadays when I show the model on a screen I usually colour the circles red, blue and green, for light (not pigment) refracts into these three primary colours. It is a way of suggesting that the three circles form a universal model. In whatever field you are, at whatever level of leadership – team leader, operational leader or strategic leader – there are three things that you should always be thinking about: *task, team* and *individual*.

Keeping in mind those three primary colours, we can make an analogy with what is happening when we watch a television programme: the full-colour moving pictures are made up of dots of those three primary and (in the overlapping areas) three secondary colours. It is only when you stand well back from the complex moving and talking picture of life at work that you begin to see the underlying pattern of the three circles. Of course, they are not always so balanced and clear as the model suggests, but they are nonetheless always there.

 Can I think of three examples where something that happened in one of the circles had symptoms or knock-on effects in the other two circles?

Idea 68: Eight functions of leadership

At whatever level of leadership, task, team and individual needs must be continually thought about. To achieve the common task, maintain teamwork and satisfy individuals, certain functions have to be performed. A *function* is what leaders *do* as opposed to a *quality*, which is an aspect of what they *are*.

These functions (the *functional approach* to leadership, also called *action-centred leadership*) are:

1   Defining the task
2   Planning
3   Briefing
4   Controlling and coordinating
5   Evaluating
6   Supporting
7   Motivating
8   Setting an example

Leadership functions in relation to task, team and individual can be represented by this diagram.

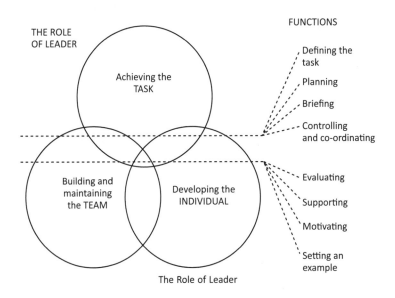

The Role of Leader

These leadership functions need to be handled with excellence and this is achieved by performing the functions with increasing skills.

Where the task is essentially a creative one, the more freedom you can give to the group and each individual, the better. Freedom within the bounds or limits you outline is a necessary condition for creativity.

In particular, the functions of *planning, controlling and coordinating* and *evaluating* need to be done with a sensitive touch. Your real job is to create a climate that is conducive to creative thinking, so don't be heavy-handed or over-controlling.

Setting an example is always relevant. If you are creative and innovative yourself in your approach to the common task, your team will be infected by the same spirit. Trust in that law. 'It is certain,' wrote Shakespeare in *King Henry IV*, 'that either wise bearing or ignorant carriage is caught, as men take diseases, therefore let men take heed of their company.'

 Which is my strongest function? And which is the function I most need to improve?

Idea 69: The decision-making continuum

If people are of one heart, even the yellow earth can become gold.

Chinese proverb

From the leadership perspective, a key issue is how far you should make all of the decisions, or all of a given decision, yourself or how far you should share this essential work with your team. Let's look at the options.

Use of authority by the leader

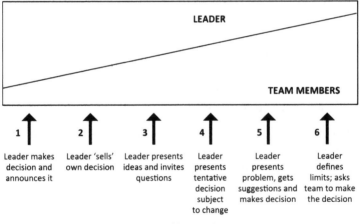

Decision Making Continuum

There is a lot to be said for moving as far to the right end of the continuum as you can. The key principle is that the more people share in decisions that affect their working life, the more they are motivated to carry them out.

That consideration, however, has to be balanced against the fact that the wider you open the door of the Inn of Decision, the less control you have of the outcome. The team may make a plan that, although meeting the boundary conditions or requirements you have specified, is not the way you would have done it yourself. Can you live with that?

Just where you should decide to make a decision on the continuum depends on several key factors, notably the time available and the competence level of the team members. There is no one right answer or 'style', as the academics used to call it.

The best leaders are consistent – you know where you stand with them and they are in many respects predictable. But when it comes to decision making they are infinitely flexible. So a good leader, working with individuals or teams, will operate at different points on the scale during a given day.

As a creative leader, what you are essentially doing is connecting up a potential or actual opportunity or problem with the fertile mind of your team as a whole – the so-called 'wisdom of crowds' – and of the individuals who comprise it.

Think of yourself as a catalyst. If you mix oxygen and hydrogen together you get gas. If you want *water*, the mother of life on earth, you need an electric spark. Your job is to be the vital spark, the catalyst that triggers off a train of truly adventurous and creative thinking.

Idea 70: Seven qualities of leadership

A leader does not only have leadership qualities, they have the appropriate knowledge and skill to lead a group to achieve its ends *willingly*.

Personality and character cannot be left out of leadership, however. There are certain generic leadership traits. The following is an indicative list, no more than that:

1   *Enthusiasm* – try naming a leader without it!
2   *Integrity* – meaning both personal wholeness and sticking to values outside yourself, primarily goodness and truth. Integrity makes people trust a leader.
3   *Toughness* – demanding, with high standards, resilient, tenacious and with the aim of being respected (not necessarily popular).
4   *Fairness* – impartial, rewarding/penalizing performance without 'favourites', treating individuals differently but equally. Firm but fair.
5   *Warmth* – the heart as well as the mind being engaged, loving what is being done and caring for people. 'Cold fish' do not make good leaders.
6   *Humility* – the opposite of arrogance, being a listener and without an overpowering ego.
7   *Confidence* – not over-confident (which leads to arrogance), but with a calm self-confidence. People know whether you have or have not got it.

If you put these qualities to work, you will create a climate that draws out the best in your team and its individual members, including their creativeness of mind. But remember that no one can lead others on a journey if they are not prepared to make the journey themselves. In the adventure of ideas, lead from the front!

In our complex and interdependent world, vulnerable to disruption, few things are more important than the quality and credibility of leaders.

Unattributed

Idea 71: Leadership qualities test

In testing whether or not you have the basic qualities of leadership, you should ask yourself these questions:

- Do I possess the seven qualities outlined in Idea 70?
- Have I demonstrated that I am a responsible person?
- Do I like the responsibility and the rewards of leadership?
- Am I well known for my enthusiasm at work?
- Have I ever been described as having integrity?
- Do I have the toughness and firmness of a good leader? Can I expect and demand the best from people – beginning with myself?
- Am I firm but fair in my dealings with both the team as a whole and each individual member?
- Can I show that people think of me as a warm and kind person?
- Am I an active and socially participative person?
- Do I have the self-confidence to take criticism, indifference and/or unpopularity from others?
- Do I have practical imagination and do I encourage it in those who work with me?
- Can I control my emotions and moods or do I let them control me?
- Have I been dishonest or less than straight with people who work for me over the past six months?
- Do I lead by example when it comes to being willing to consider and explore new ideas?

Creative leadership, like all forms of leadership, depends on the situation. So you need to ask yourself if you are right for the kind of situation where new ideas and new ways of doing things really matter:

◆ Are my interests, aptitudes and temperament suited to my current field of work?

◆ If not, can I identify one that would better suit where I would emerge as a leader?

◆ Do I have the 'authority of knowledge' in my current field (and have I acquired all the necessary professional and specialist skills through training that I could have done at this point in my career)?

◆ Am I experienced in more than one field/industry/function?

◆ Am I interested in fields adjacent and relevant to my own?

◆ Do I read situations well and am I flexible in my approach to changes within my field?

◆ Do I have a 'tolerance for ambiguity' – an ability to put up with the uncertainties and risks involved in all creative and innovative thinking?

Remember that your position does not give you the right to command. It only lays upon you the duty of so living your life that others may receive your orders without being humiliated.

Dag Hammarskjöld, second Secretary-General of
the United Nations (writing to himself)

Idea 72: Humility in action

Excellence and humility go hand in hand. The best leaders are not self-centred egotists. They put their role and responsibilities as leaders first – the dignity of their office, not of themselves. They serve people through that role. Their eyes are on truth, not on self.

A leader is best
When people barely know that he exists,
Not so good when people obey and acclaim him,
Worst when they despise him.
'Fail to honour people,
They fail to honour you';
But of a good leader, who talks little,
When his work is done, his aim fulfilled,
They will all say, 'We did this ourselves.'
Lao Tzu, sixth century BCE

 The best leaders lack vanity and self-importance.

Idea 73: Five qualities of creative leadership

Don't try to get your wild geese to fly in formation.

Thomas J Watson, founder of IBM

Apart from fulfilling the generic role of leader in the shape or form required in your field (see Ideas 66 to 69), you need to develop some extra characteristics if you wish to be successful at leading creative teams. Now is your opportunity to adopt them if they are not already part of your philosophy. Here is an indicative list:

A willingness to bend rules

'Mr Edison, please tell me what laboratory rules you want me to observe,' asked a newly appointed colleague on his first day at work.

'There *ain't* no rules around here,' replied Edison emphatically. 'We are trying to accomplish something.'

Rules and systems have their place, but they can really obstruct the process of innovation. A leader, as a member of the management team, should respect rules and procedures, but he or she should not think like a bureaucrat. Sometimes instructional dyslexia, the inability to read rules, is a strength rather than a weakness.

Rules can sometimes be stretched where they cannot be broken. Without this you end up being bogged down in organizational treacle – or, as Charles Dickens said, 'Skewered through and through with office-pens and bound hand and foot with red tape.'

Remember how Admiral Lord Nelson once famously put his telescope to his blind eye to avoid carrying out an unproductive order? Having a blind eye can be a strength on occasion, not a weakness. Don't be afraid to use your initiative when occasion demands it.

An ability to work with half-baked ideas

Ideas seldom leap into the world fully formed and ready to go. They are more like newborn babies, struggling and gasping for life.

Leaders who facilitate team creativity demonstrate by example the value of listening to half-developed ideas and building on them if they have merit. They hesitate before dismissing an ill-formed idea or an imperfect proposal, for it may contain the germ of something really useful.

It follows that team creativity in groups and organizations calls for listening leaders.

An ability to respond quickly

To continue the newborn baby analogy, some new ideas or projects need sustenance quickly if they are going to survive. Leaders who mean business about creativity and innovation should have a flair for spotting potential winners. But that is not enough.

The innovative organization must have leaders who are able to commit resources and not always have to defer *everything* to committees or upwards to a higher authority. Remember the saying: 'Nothing is impossible unless it is sent to a committee.' Committees have a habit of quietly smothering newborn ideas.

Being able to allocate or obtain small resources now may be far better than being able to summon mighty resources in a year's time when it's too late. That is why some organizations appoint 'project sponsors', senior managers who are able to secure resources at a high level quickly for promising ideas.

Personal enthusiasm

Only leaders who are highly motivated themselves will motivate others. Enthusiasm is contagious. Moreover, enthusiastic leaders and colleagues tend to be intellectually stimulating ones.

'Man never rises to great truths without enthusiasm,' wrote French essayist Vauvenargues. Innovation usually deals in small truths or incremental improvements, but the same principle holds good.

A tolerance for failure

As Nobel Prize winner Sydney Brenner, then Director of the Laboratory of Molecular Biology at Cambridge, once said to me: 'If you want to innovate, give a person a chance. Innovation is gambling. Once you play safe you are lost.' In other words, you have to be willing to accept an element of risk, for without risk there would be no mistakes, no errors and no failures.

Eliminating freedom is the biggest mistake of all: freedom alone breeds innovation and entrepreneurial success. Mistakes are a by-product of progress. Learn from them, but do not dwell on them.

'If you have not worked on the edge of failure, you have not worked on the edge of real success.'

Creative leadership means the mind of leadership that encourages, stimulates and guides the process of innovation from beginning to end. The challenge of innovation is largely the challenge of leading creative people. Have you faced, understood and accepted that challenge?

> *Not geniuses but ordinary men and women require profound stimulation, incentive towards creative effort, and the nurture of great hopes.*
>
> John Collier, *English poet*

Twelve Greatest Ideas for Motivating the Creative Individual

Idea 74: Selecting creative people

> *It is the human being who counts.*
> *Call on gold, gold does not respond.*
> *Call on clothes, clothes do not respond.*
>
> Ghanaian proverb

As a manager you need to understand how creative or innovative individuals think and what they want. For innovation will not happen unless the men and women who work with you are motivated. They must *want* to innovate.

According to my Fifty-Fifty Principle, 50 per cent of motivation lies within us in the shape of our response to inner needs, drives and values. The other 50 per cent depends on our environment, especially the leadership that we encounter within it.

As a corollary of that rule, it is important first to get your selection procedures right. Choose people who have the seeds of the future within them. The first step in any form of team building is to choose the right people. That is a vital principle to bear in mind if you wish to encourage innovation – and sustain it.

Like Dr Livingstone, in his inimitable way, you should develop an eye for the more adventurous and more independently minded person. As movie mogul Sam Goldwyn put it, 'I don't want any yes-men around me. I want everyone to tell the truth even if it costs them their jobs!'

When it comes to innovation there has to be a premium on youth. Young people tend to be more future-oriented. After all, most of their life will be spent in the future. Moreover, the fact that young people lack experience (which could almost be defined as the knowledge of what does not work) inclines them to be ready to experiment. They have less mental luggage in the form of preconceptions or assumptions. The older we grow in years, the more cautious and the more conservative we tend to become. You can see why Napoleon once mused that the art of government was not to let people grow old in their jobs.

Any innovative organization must therefore have a bias towards attracting intelligent and creative young people. Of course, intellectual qualities are not enough, for industry needs *doers* – people who can make things happen – rather than merely *thinkers*.

There are plenty of good ideas around. The real issue is whether or not you have the people in your team or organization who are willing to put new ideas to work – in other words, to innovate.

Creative people are attracted by creative environments and opportunities. Therefore, as a manager you need to make sure that your organization has the right colours to attract them and that you advertise these attractions in the job market or to individuals you have identified.

How will you recognize creativity? It is rather like height, weight and strength. We vary considerably in these dimensions, but all of us have some height, some weight and some strength. Thus there is a certain amount of potential for creative thinking in all of us, but some people are clearly more creative than others. Your organization needs its fair share of this creative talent.

You can usually identify some general characteristics. Creative people tend to be more open and flexible than their less creative neighbours. They bring a freshness of mind to problems. They have usually exhibited the courage to be different and to think for themselves. 'Give me the young man,' said *Treasure Island* author Robert Louis Stevenson, 'who has brains enough to make a fool of himself.'

Exercise

You are about to interview someone for a job that especially requires the ability to have new ideas. It requires a fresh mind and an innovative spirit. Place the following personal qualities or attributes in order of importance:

Numeracy

Lack of interest in small details

Curiosity

Verbal skills

Sensitivity

Wide-ranging interests

Enthusiasm

Independence

A good analytical mind

A flexible mind

Scepticism

Orientation to achievement

Humour

Persistence

Self-confidence

Non-conformity

Add *three* characteristics that you feel are missing from the list.

When Dr Livingstone was working in Africa, a group of friends wrote: 'We would like to send other men to you. Have you found a good road into your area yet?'

According to a member of his family, Dr Livingstone sent this message in reply: 'If you have men who will only come if they know there is a good road, I don't want them. I want men who will come if there is no road at all.'

A house is made up of individual bricks. The quality of an innovative organization depends ultimately and largely on the quality of the people you employ. Machines do not have new ideas. Computers cannot create. Money alone cannot create a satisfied customer.

Idea 75: Ten things a creative person ought to be

You *can* learn to be more creative. Here are some suggestions.

1 Think beyond the invisible frameworks that surround problems and situations.
2 Recognize when assumptions are being made and challenge them.
3 Spot blinkered thinking and widen the field of vision (to draw on the experiences of other individuals and businesses).
4 Develop and adapt ideas from more than one source.
5 Practise serendipity (finding valuable and agreeable things when not particularly seeking them). Having a wide attention span and range of interests is important.
6 'Transfer technology' from one field to another.
7 Be open and prepared to use chance or unpredictable things and events to advantage.
8 Explore thought processes and the key elements of your mind at work in analyzing, valuing and synthesizing.
9 Use your depth mind (the unconscious mind), for example by sleeping on a problem to generate creative solutions.
10 Note down thoughts and ideas that apparently drop into your mind unsolicited so that they are not forgotten.

Discovery consists of seeing what everyone has seen and thinking what nobody has thought.

Idea 76: How to recruit and retain creative people

To help you recruit creative people, appreciate and look for these characteristics:

- ◆ Of high general intelligence.
- ◆ Strongly motivated.
- ◆ Stimulated by challenge.
- ◆ Vocational in their attitude to work.
- ◆ Able to hold contradictory ideas together in creative tension.
- ◆ Curious, with good listening and observing skills.
- ◆ Able to think for themselves, independent in thought.
- ◆ Neither an introvert nor an extrovert, but rather in the middle.
- ◆ Interested in many areas and things.

Creative individuals thrive if they are:

- ◆ Appreciated and receive recognition.
- ◆ Given freedom to work in their area(s) of greatest interest.
- ◆ Allowed contact with stimulating colleagues.
- ◆ Given stimulating projects to work on.
- ◆ Free to make mistakes.

To retain creative people, you need to ensure that their creativity continues to thrive in the right environment, but also that financially they are flexibly and well rewarded and given the freedom to operate and work without being stifled by excess bureaucracy.

The quality of an innovative organization depends ultimately on the quality of the people you employ.

Idea 77: Seven obstacles to creativity

There are a number of obstacles that inhibit creativity. The seven main ones are:

1   Negativity.
2   Fear of failure.
3   Lack of quality thinking time.
4   Over-conformance with rules and regulations.
5   Making assumptions.
6   Applying too much logic.
7   Thinking you are not creative.

These obstacles can be seen in this identikit profile of the non-creative person, someone who is:

◆ Not able to think positively about problems (and does not see them as opportunities).
◆ Too busy or stressed to think objectively or at all.
◆ Very self-critical.
◆ Timid in putting forward a new idea (fearing ridicule).
◆ Viewed as a conformist by friends or colleagues.
◆ Prone to apply logic as a first and last resort.
◆ Sceptical that many people are capable of being creative.
◆ Unable to think laterally.
◆ Uninspired even when confronted with a new idea.

On the other hand, creativity can be encouraged in people (including yourself) by exploring some of the qualities and characteristics of creative thinkers and the activities and steps that can be undertaken to improve the processes involved.

How many of the seven obstacles to creativity do I recognize in myself?

How am I going to overcome them?

Which are the easiest ones to deal with first?

Idea 78: Characteristics of innovators

The best of men are but men at their best.

English proverb

Creative or innovative people can usually be recognized by having a pattern of characteristics like those represented in the list below. Such people do not make natural organizational men and women, so your organization needs a certain psychological maturity to recruit them in the first place. Creative people can make uncomfortable companions, but can you do without them?

Here is a list of characteristics to look for when studying references, biographical data or during interviews:

Some qualities of creative people

General intelligence	Powers of analyzing, synthesizing and valuing, as well as the ability to store and recall information.
High self-motivation	A high degree of autonomy, self-sufficiency and self-direction. Creative people enjoy the challenge. They like to pit themselves against problems or opportunities in which their own efforts can be the deciding factor. 'There is no greater joy in life,' said the inventor Sir Barnes Wallis, 'than first proving that a thing is impossible and then showing how it can be done.' Creative people tend to be vocational in their attitude to work.
Negative capability	The ability to hold many ideas – often apparently contradictory ones – together in creative tension, without reaching for premature resolution of ambiguity. Hence, the capability of occasionally reaching a richer synthesis.
Curiosity	Sustained curiosity and powers of observation. Creative-minded people are usually good listeners.

Some qualities of creative people

Independence of mind	Marked independence of judgement. Resilience in the teeth of group pressures towards conformity in thinking. Seeing things as others do, but also as they do not. Thinking for oneself; thinking from first principles, not getting information out of books.
Wide interests	A broad range of interests, including usually those with a creative dimension.

Selection is – or ought to be – a two-way process. Before you take on creative people you should check whether or not you have the environment (including leadership) in which their talents will flourish. It is not much good hiring people if they are only going to become frustrated.

> If my organization is one that frustrates creative and innovative individuals, what does that say about my leadership and that of my colleagues?

Know your own strengths

Creative thinkers are clearly stronger in synthesizing, imagining and holistic thinking than others. But the best of them are equally strong in analyzing ability and the faculty of valuing or judging. It is this combination of mental strengths, supported by some important personal qualities or characteristics, that makes for a formidable creative mind.

Idea 79: Team creativity

Many ideas grow better when transplanted into another mind than in the one where they sprang up.

Oliver Wendell Holmes, American judge

A new idea almost invariably comes from an individual, but it takes a team to turn it into something really useful. From this principle, as stated thus, it would be easy to dichotomize the process. The individual who has the new idea is being *creative*, you might say, while the group or organization that develops it is being *innovative*. But this would be an over-simplification.

What the individual usually comes up with is a half-formed idea. That is often, incidentally, the result of a preliminary discussion with colleagues. Then that half-baked idea is creatively developed by one or more others working like a team. The whole process is best called *team creativity*.

The Japanese economy has been transformed by the practical application of that concept. As individuals the Japanese are not noted for their creativity. Indeed, Japanese culture, especially its educational system, has traditionally played down individuality. 'If a nail stands up, it will be hammered down,' declares a Japanese proverb bluntly. That is not a spirit that develops much creativity in individuals.

But in groups the Japanese have shown themselves to be remarkably innovative. In the West, in comparison, we may have been over-emphasizing the role of the individual in the context of creativity.

If you look closely at creative thinking, even apparently solitary creators such as authors, inventors or artists, there is a considerable input from others before and after the emergence of a seminal idea. Being human and anxious for personal recognition, individuals often over-emphasize their own parts. And Western society conspires by recognizing and rewarding individuals rather than teams for creative work.

Team creativity points to the fact that more than one person is involved in any significant act of creative thinking. This is even more apparent when it comes to innovation. To develop a product or service from an idea, however mature, self-evidently requires creative teamwork.

Idea 80: Brainstorming

Brainstorming in its wider sense is a concerted intellectual explora-
tion of a problem by generating and discussing spontaneous ideas
about it.

There are four simple rules or guidelines for brainstorming:

1 *Suspend judgement* – criticism of ideas should be with-
   held until later.
2 *Freewheel* – the crazier the idea the better; it's easier to
   tone down than to think up.
3 *Quantity* – the more ideas pile up, the more likelihood
   there is of winners.
4 *Cross-fertilize* – in addition to contributing ideas, participants are free to suggest how another person's idea can
   be turned into a better idea; or how two or more ideas
   can be combined into still another idea.

Notice that the brainstorming technique rests on the principle of
separating *synthesizing* artificially from *analyzing* and *valuing* (see
Idea 9). But ideas do have to be subjected to rigorous evaluation at
some stage or other. To be able to give such criticism effectively, and
to receive it, is an art that has to be learnt.

There are few people who have participated in brainstorming sessions who have not experienced a 'chain reaction' when minds are
really warmed up, and a spark from one mind lights up a lot of ideas
in others like a string of firecrackers.

Association of ideas clearly comes into play, so that an idea put into
words stirs your imagination or memory towards another idea, while
at the same time it stimulates associative connections in other people's minds, often at a subconscious level.

Case study: Pilkington Brothers

Pilkington Brothers Limited in the UK had a technical problem . . . During the final inspection of sheet glass, small globules of water were identified by the inspection machine as flaws in the glass. A brainstorming session produced 29 ideas in less than five minutes. After research and development, three of these were used in the system, which solved the problem.

Case study: H J Heinz

H J Heinz in the USA had a marketing problem . . . The company wanted to get sales promotional material to consumers more quickly. Brainstorming produced 195 ideas. After evaluation, eight were used immediately. A member of Heinz, when talking about another brainstorming session, said: 'Brainstorming generated more and better ideas than our special committee produced in 10 meetings.'

It's always best not to judge other people's ideas too soon or too critically. An angry banker once told Thomas Edison to 'get that toy out of my office!' – so Edison took his invention (the phonograph) somewhere else.

You can, of course, apply the brainstorming principle in your own thinking or informally in conversation with friends. Give free rein to your spontaneous ideas.

'If at first the idea is not absurd, then there is no hope for it.'
Albert Einstein

Exercise

Take a pair of scissors and list 50 new functions or uses for them – apart from the primary function of cutting things. You have 10 minutes.

Write your ideas down. If you get stuck, here is a practical tip: go back and build on your first 10 ideas. The world record is 596 ideas. If you list over 100 ideas you are doing exceptionally well.

Idea 81: How to lead a brainstorming session

The best way to get a good idea is to get lots of ideas.

Linus Pauling, American chemist

No more than 10 people should be involved in a brainstorming session. Some may know about the field, others may not – a mixture of both is desirable. They should have been introduced to the brainstorming technique before the meeting and ideally have some practice in it. When you run the sessions:

◆ Remind participants of the four rules, especially the first. As one discussion leader said:

If you try to get hot and cold water out of the same tap at the same time, you will get only tepid water. And if you try to criticize and *create at the same, you can't turn on either* cold *enough criticism or* hot *enough ideas. So let's stick solely to* ideas – *let's cut out* all *criticism during this session.*

◆ Define the real problem or opportunity (using your analytical and briefing skills).
◆ Help people to understand the problem or opportunity by highlighting the background information and history.
◆ Clarify the aim in a succinct sentence: 'In how many ways can we . . . ?'
◆ Have a brief warm-up session, using a common problem or object.
◆ Brainstorm 70 ideas in 20 minutes, or a similar target. One person should write up the ideas on a flipchart. *Do not edit*. Ideas should not be elaborated or defended, just quickly stated and recorded.

◆ Allow time for silent reflection. Check that no critical remarks are made.
◆ Encourage cross-fertilization at this stage.
◆ Establish criteria for selecting the feasible ideas. Choose the best. (Here you are inviting participants to switch on their valuing faculty or mode of thinking.)
◆ Reverse brainstorm: 'In how many ways can this idea fail?'

About 40 minutes is the optimum time for a brainstorming session. But you should ask the participants to go on considering the problem and let you have further suggestions. Remember that they have programmed their depth minds by the brainstorming session, and other ideas will come to them unexpectedly.

Case study: Jigsaw puzzles

A leading US firm of jigsaw puzzle-makers held a brainstorming session to think up ideas for new puzzles. It produced some worthy ideas, but nothing brilliant. A month later, one of the participants went to see an exhibition of Tutankhamun's treasures in Washington, DC. The gold mask of the pharaoh struck him as a great jigsaw puzzle idea! He was right – it broke all records for jigsaw puzzle sales in the United States.

Winston Churchill was a leader noted for the sheer quantity of his ideas, especially during the Second World War. Although he pressed his strategic ideas with his vigorous powers of persuasion and formidable command of the English language, he always submitted ultimately to the professional evaluation of his cabinet of ministers and committee of military chiefs of staff. He once said: 'No idea is so outlandish that it should not be considered with a searching but at the same time a steady eye.' Do you agree?

Idea 82: Team creativity in action

The invention of Scotch Tape is a highlight in the story of 3M, the Minnesota corporation that grew from being a maker of mediocre sandpaper into an international conglomerate.

The salesmen who visited the auto plants noticed that workers painting new two-toned cars were having trouble keeping the colours from running together.

Richard G Drew, a young 3M lab technician, came up with the answer: masking tape, the company's first tape. Drew then figured out how to put adhesive on it, and Scotch Tape was born, initially for industrial packaging.

It didn't really begin to roll until another imaginative 3M hero, John Borden, a sales manager, created a dispenser with a built-in blade.

You can see that members of this company had learnt to build on one another's ideas. The process of innovation is largely incremental. It requires the efforts and contributions of a team if an idea is to be brought successfully to the market place. Rarely is an idea marketable just as it is conceived in someone's mind.

The ability to suspend judgement for a time – both as an individual thinker and as a team member – is important. The ability to build on other people's ideas, improving or combining them, is also essential.

But these two abilities do not exhaust the repertoire of skills required in a member of a truly innovative organization. The ability to criticize in an acceptable and diplomatic manner, in the right way, at the right time and in the right place, has to be developed.

Here team creativity transcends brainstorming, which, by definition, eliminates criticism. It is really no more than a snapshot of one phase of creative teamwork. Analyzing and evaluating are equally necessary phases in the shared mental process.

Again, as in the case of synthesizing and imagining, when it comes to analyzing and evaluating there is a musical relationship between the individual thinker and the group. The 'solo' thinker may suggest themes developed by a section of the orchestra; another soloist may take forwards a refrain identified by the players as a whole.

Idea 83: How to criticize other people's new ideas

A new idea is delicate. It can be killed by a sneer or a yawn; it can be stabbed to death by a quip and worried to death by a frown on the right man's brow.

Charles Brower, American copywriter

The management of criticism is almost as important as the management of innovation. Make no mistake, criticism has to be done. Expensive mistakes may occur, leading organizations up blind and profitless alleyways, if ideas are not evaluated rigorously at the right time.

Henry Ford used to content himself with just three questions:

1   Is it needed?
2   Is it practical?
3   Is it commercial?

These three key questions and their satellites do have to be pressed home hard in commercial and industrial organizations in the right way, at the right time and in the right place. Don't confuse the art of the possible with the art of the profitable. Nevertheless, these questions should not be applied prematurely in the creative process.

Sometimes, however, ideas have to evolve quite far before any practical and commercial use becomes apparent. But tested they must be by others at various stages of their life history. The good ones are those that can jump the hurdles of criticism.

Testing or criticizing other people's new ideas – and being on the receiving end of that treatment – is often not a pleasant process. It can be downright demoralizing to the receiver. We have to learn the 'manners of conversation'. In our context of criticism, that means learning to express our views with tact and diplomacy.

Case study: Francis Crick

Francis Crick, co-discoverer with James Watson of the double helix, describes two valuable lessons about criticism in his biography, *What Mad Pursuit! A Personal View of Scientific Discovery* (1988). He had joined the group studying molecular biology in the Cavendish Laboratory at Cambridge, which formed the nucleus later for the independent Laboratory for Molecular Biology. The group was under the general supervision of Sir Lawrence Bragg, a Nobel laureate for his work on X-ray crystallography.

At this time Crick was already over 30, with no research record to speak of. But he told the group that they were all wasting their time for, according to his analyses, almost all the methods they were pursuing had no chance of success. Bragg soon became very annoyed with the brash young American. Crick reports:

> *There was some justification for his annoyance. A group of people engaged in a difficult and somewhat uncertain undertaking are not helped by persistent negative criticism from one of their number. It destroys the mood of confidence necessary to carry through such a hazardous enterprise to a successful conclusion. But equally it is useless to persist in a course of action that is bound to fail, especially if an alternative method exists. As it has turned out, I was completely correct in all my criticisms with one exception . . .*
>
> *I received another lesson when Perutz described his results to a small group of x-ray crystallographers from different parts of Britain assembled in the Cavendish.*

After his presentation, Bernal rose to comment on it. I regarded Bernal as a genius. For some reason I had acquired the idea that all geniuses behaved badly. I was therefore surprised to hear him praise Perutz in the most genial way for his courage in undertaking such a difficult and, at that time, unprecedented task and for his thoroughness and persistence in carrying it through. Only then did Bernal venture to express, in the nicest possible way, some reservations he had about the Patterson method and this example of it in particular.

I learned that if you have something critical to say about a piece of scientific work, it is better to say it firmly but nicely and to preface it with praise of any good aspects of it. I only wish I had always stuck to this useful rule. Unfortunately I have sometimes been carried away by my impatience and expressed myself too briskly and in too devastating a manner.

Idea 84: Building on ideas

Every fool can see what is wrong. See what is good in it!

British Prime Minister Winston Churchill,
speaking to his cabinet colleagues

At the core of team creativity is the capacity to build on or improve other people's ideas, and to subject your own ideas to the same process. 'The typical eye sees the 10 per cent bad of an idea,' writes American inventor Charles F Kettering, 'and overlooks the 90 per cent good.'

Some skills in generating ideas:

Questions/statements	Notes
Bringing in ideas 'Bob, you have had experience in several other industries, how did they tackle this problem?'	Meets individual needs as well as the task.
Stimulating ideas 'Imagine we were starting from scratch again. How would we do it?'	Brains are like car engines. They need warming up by outrageous ideas or thought-provoking suggestions.
Building on ideas 'Can't we develop the idea behind Mary's suggestion of cutting down the number of files? Could we use the computer more? How else can we improve our information storage system?'	Entails seeing the positive idea or principle in a suggestion and taking it further.
Spreading ideas 'We can also include Jim's suggestion about time-keeping and Mary's point about safety in the plan.'	Helps to develop a team solution. A creative process of weaving separate threads and loose ends together into a whole.

Questions/statements	Notes
Accepting while rejecting ideas 'Mike's proposal is an interesting and helpful one, but it would take us rather too long so we must leave it on one side for the present.'	You are accepting Mike, but rejecting his plan in a gracious way. He will not be resentful, and may come up with the winning idea next time.

Idea 85: Expectations of creative people

Three cobblers with their wits combined, equal Zhuge Liang the master mind.

Chinese proverb (Zhuge Liang, a famous statesman and strategist, was chief minister of the state of Shu 220–280 BCE)

If you recruit or select people with above-average creative ability for your team or organization, you will find that they tend to be looking for certain compatible characteristics in you and your organization as well.

Here, in order of importance, are some of the more important environmental factors in stimulating or encouraging creativity:

1 *Recognition and appreciation* – because the results of creative work are often postponed for a long time (many geniuses received no recognition in their lifetimes), creative people stand in special need of encouragement and appreciation. The recognition of the value or worth of their contribution is especially important to them, particularly if it comes from those whose opinions they respect.

2 *Freedom to work in areas of greatest interest* – while the predominantly analytical person concentrates and focuses down, the creative person wanders in every possible or feasible direction. Freedom to move is a necessary condition of creative work. A creative person tends to be most effective if allowed to choose the area of work, and the problems or opportunities within that area, which arouses the deepest interest.

3 *Contacts with stimulating colleagues* – 'two heads are better than one' says an ancient Greek proverb. Creative

people need conversation with colleagues in order to think, not merely for social intercourse.

4   *Stimulating projects to work on* – along with a congenial and appreciative environment and the opportunity for appropriate recognition by their professional peers inside and outside the organization, stimulating projects, be they opportunities or problems, are especially attractive.

5   *Freedom to make mistakes* – errors are inescapable in innovative work. The climate should be such that they are not all used to inflict immediate and permanent damage on one's professional career.

Some practical implications

'An essential aspect of creativity is not being afraid to fail,' said Edward Lane, inventor of the Polaroid camera. It is the *fear* of failure that does the most damage. You need to create a climate in which those who fail responsibly are not penalized. Irresponsible failure is another matter.

Successful innovative companies such as 3M lean over backwards to give individuals as much freedom as possible. You don't provide children with colouring books and then warn them to stay inside the lines of the drawings. For creative managers to expect their creative team members to stay inside the lines is a contradiction in terms.

Such inhibiting boundaries may be job descriptions, detailed instructions on how to do something, or any other unconsciously restrictive practices. If you place too many fences around people, they can easily become like sheep in a pasture. And how many patents are assigned to sheep?

> '*Recognition is the oxygen of the human spirit.*'

Follow-up test

Your role as creative leader

☐ Are you clear about the generic role and responsibilities of leaders?

☐ 'You can be appointed a manager, but you are not a leader until your appointment is ratified in the hearts and minds of those who work with you.' Do you agree? When was the last time someone referred to you as a leader?

☐ Can you think of how you can develop the five qualities of creative leadership within yourself?

   1 A willingness to bend rules
   2 An ability to respond quickly
   3 An ability to work with half-baked ideas
   4 Personal enthusiasm
   5 A tolerance for failure

☐ Do you lead by example when it comes to the willingness to consider and explore new ideas?

☐ Are you able to create a climate that is conducive to creative thinking?

Motivating the creative individual

☐ Do you look for imagination when selecting your team members?

☐ List three ways in which you have raised the level of team creativity in your group.

   1
   2
   3

- ☐ Do you make use of the brainstorming technique when the situation or problem invites it?
- ☐ If brainstorming doesn't seem to work, do you always check to see if it isn't due to some failure in your own leadership?
- ☐ Do group brainstorming sessions, in your experience, lead to much more individual creative thinking around the office or factory? If so, can you give examples?
- ☐ Have you a shopping list of the main specific but open-ended problems and opportunities that face you in your area of responsibility?
- ☐ Does each first-line team leader have a similar shopping list?
- ☐ Does your organization make sufficient use of project groups or creative thinking task forces?
- ☐ When it comes to avoiding negative criticism and building on ideas, do you lead by example?

What a man dislikes in his superiors, let him not display in his treatment of his inferiors.

Tsang Sin, *Confucian philosopher*

PART FIVE

Turning Ideas into Improved Products and Services

What is honoured in a country will be cultivated there.

Plato, Greek philosopher

Innovation is the lifeblood of any organization today. Nothing holds back a company – and the individuals working in it – more than a lack of interest in positive change. You cannot stand still: you go either backwards or forwards.

Innovation requires a blend of new ideas, teamwork and leadership. Apart from creativity and the ability to get things done, however, it also calls for a sound commercial or entrepreneurial sense at all levels of the organization.

Innovation should be customer driven as well as ideas driven. The success of innovative projects therefore depends on both your individual characteristics as a leader and manager, and the climate or orientation of the whole organization.

In today's competitive world, success flows to the organization that does today what you were thinking about doing tomorrow!

You need to be able to lead and manage innovation. The guidelines in Part Five cover the essentials of what you have to do to help teams develop new ideas, the ways in which you can build an innovative organization, one that can take your creative ideas into the market place and turn them into profit.

'As a business leader, my personal product is improvement.'

Eight Greatest Ideas for Building Innovative Organizations

Idea 86: Real commitment from the top

Without real commitment from the top, real innovation will be defeated again and again by the policies, procedures and rituals of almost any large organization.

Unattributed

The attitudes, personal qualities and skills of leaders in organizations stand out as a group of vital ingredients in innovation. Be they team leaders or first-line managers, operational leaders or leaders at the strategic level, the managers of an enterprise can do a great deal to encourage creativity.

Without exception, all the most effective leaders I have ever known create a sense of *esprit de corps*, a team spirit that makes even the most arduous or the most humdrum work exciting. The synergy created supports and sustains the individuals in the group.

At chief executive level, the successful leader's team will be a small group of senior operational leaders and key heads of staff functions who can think strategically with him or her, help to change the corporate culture towards greater creative teamwork, and devise the means of getting extraordinary results from the individuals who make up the workforce.

The first and most important necessary condition, of course, is that the chief executive and the strategic leadership team show *real commitment to team creativity and innovation*. That means not only personal encouragement and example, but also making resources available.

Innovation, then, calls for good leadership throughout an enterprise. Good leadership ought to stem from the chief executive. It is his or her prime responsibility to manage change. As the Roman author Publilius Syrus said, 'Anyone can hold the helm when the sea is calm.'

The role of strategic leader

The generic role of *strategic leader*, in response to the three areas of need (see Idea 65), has now been successfully broken down into functions. The seven key functions of a strategic leader are:

1 Providing a clear sense of direction.
2 Strategic thinking and strategic planning.
3 Making it happen.
4 Relating the parts of the organization to the whole, so that it works as a team.
5 Relating the organization to allies and partners, and to society as a whole.
6 Releasing the corporate energy and creativity within the organization.
7 Selecting and developing today's and tomorrow's leaders.

You can see that having ideas oneself, and encouraging creativity in others, is part of the job description. The organization is on a journey and it requires direction. A journey means change. If the leadership gets it right, it will be a journey towards *desirable* change.

'Without a leadership team at the top that values product quality, new ideas and innovation, and that constantly struggles to keep organizations moving towards these guiding stars, there will be no sustained and profitable growth.' Can I think of two examples, one negative and one positive, that illustrate this principle?

Idea 87: Successful innovation

More creativity is the only way to make tomorrow better than today.

Unattributed

Innovation should not be a reactive process but part of a long-term strategy that gives direction. It needs to be fed by the dynamo of a corporate sense of purpose. Such a strategy will balance the present needs of producing and marketing *existing* goods and services – the commercial priority – with the middle- and long-term requirement of *research and development*.

A balanced and coherent strategy will enable your organization to build on its past successes and create its desired future. *It is the only sure pathway to profitable growth*.

There are always reasons for not becoming an innovative organization, not least the fact that it costs money to go down that path. But can you afford the cost of the alternative?

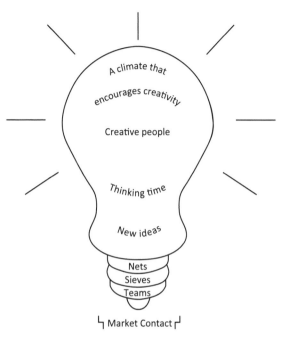

Successful Innovation

- ◆ *Nets* – the new ideas have to be netted, or harvested.
- ◆ *Sieves* – a sorting-out process is needed in order to separate the gold dust from the mud.
- ◆ *Teams* – developing modifications or improvements, and bringing new products to market, always calls for a mix of talents, skills and knowledge.

This model suggests that good new ideas are more likely to be forthcoming in an organization that encourages creative people and allows time for productive thinking. Needless to say, this requires leadership and vision to bring about and to sustain the right climate.

> *'People support what they help to create.'*

The results of successful innovation include:

◆ Stimulated team members.
◆ Delighted customers.
◆ Profitable growth.

He who dares nothing need hope for nothing.

English proverb

Idea 88: Harvesting ideas

The creative act thrives in an environment of mutual stimulation, feedback and constructive criticism – in a community of creativity.

William T Brady, US business executive

Each person who works with you is capable of generating a great many new ideas for improving the products and services of your business.

Therefore your challenge as a leader is to elicit the new ideas and fresh thinking that are potentially there in those who work for you. 'In the coldest flint there is a hot fire' says an English proverb.

One way of doing so is to introduce what could be called *innovative systems*, notably suggestion schemes and quality circles, which are designed to encourage and harvest ideas at work.

Managers who are not leaders tend to believe that all problems can be solved by introducing a system. But systems are usually only half the solution. The other half is the people running them and the people participating in them. That spells out the need for leadership at all levels, together with a sound recruitment policy coupled with a comprehensive training programme. There is no such thing as instant innovation.

In modern times the first managers who demonstrated real faith in the creativity within their people, and systematically went about harvesting ideas from the workforce, were the Japanese.

Of course, it wasn't a new idea. Henry Ford had introduced the world's first assembly line for car manufacturing in 1913. Every man on the payroll was invited to contribute ideas, and the best ones were implemented without delay. Ford and his managers created an atmosphere in which *improvement* was the real product.

Why, 100 years later, are Japanese car manufacturers outselling American ones?

The secret of Japanese success

As a special bonus for reading this book, here's a remarkable secret I came across by serendipity when speaking at an international conference in Malaysia.

The Japanese speakers and I became very friendly, and after one convivial evening I felt bold enough to ask them, 'Why do you allow so many Western visitors to tour your factories and steal your *kaizen* techniques for incremental product improvements? Why do you allow us to study your phenomenal innovation? We are competitors, you know.'

My Japanese friend smiled and replied that the answer was very simple. At my request he wrote it down for me. As a world exclusive, here it is:

貴方には出来
ないでしょう

Should your Japanese not be up to it, I have supplied a translation in the Appendix.

> *'There's a way to do it better – you just need to find it.'*

Idea 89: Suggestion schemes

In 1857 the Chance Brothers of Smethwick, surprised when their workers suggested ways of improving production and saving on materials, hit on the idea of putting a wooden box where such ideas could be posted. The scheme proved to be of immense worth to the firm and to the workers. It was the world's first suggestion scheme.

Exercise

A staff member working in the transport industry got himself into the *Guinness Book of Records* with the number of suggestions he offered during a career of over 40 years. Tick the number of ideas that you think he came up with:

Over 2,000 ☐	Over 20,000 ☐
Over 1,200 ☐	Over 8,000 ☐
Over 6,000 ☐	

The answer is in the Appendix .

The enthusiastic support of leaders at all levels is essential. Lazy managers who merely put up a box for suggestions in the work place and sit back to await a few million-dollar ideas are wasting their opportunity. Ask some pointed questions. Give people a fairly specific direction for their thinking. Our imaginations must have bones to gnaw on.

A quick response to new ideas or suggestions is also essential. Knowledge of results is always motivating. Conversely, not knowing what has happened to your bright idea for months on end is extremely demotivating and demoralizing. The system must be such that participants know fairly soon whether the organization is saying yes, no or wait.

Research suggests that people are not demotivated if their idea is rejected, provided the reasons for doing so are set out clearly and convincingly. Needless to say, even junior colleagues are in as much need of tact and diplomacy when their ideas are being rejected as scientists, managers or professional people.

'Pride is really the first thing that matters; the money comes second. To be picked out of a corporation like British Airways is really something.' So said Michael Rowlerson, winner of a national competition for suggestions in the UK, when asked about the large cash prize he received from British Airways for suggesting how to remove corrosion from the inside of undercarriage struts.

To repeat the point, the general consensus is that money is not the prime motivator when it comes to generating new ideas: recognition and sense of achievement are way ahead of it. But that should not prevent companies from giving more realistic monetary prizes, both as signs of recognition and as incentives to others.

To enjoy success, suggestion schemes need to be marketed internally. Special events, publicity, newsletters and local newspaper or radio, together with a lively and compelling promotional booklet, are all ingredients in keeping the system alive and functioning well. Never expect any system to go on working without maintenance, revision and reinspiration.

Granted these ingredients, suggestion schemes are a most valuable system for harvesting innovative ideas. At one food manufacturing company, for example, one employee, originally a butter packer, moved into design engineering as a result of a suggestion he made to redesign a machine. He was given a week off with a design engineer to put his suggestion into practice, and the redesign saved the company over £500,000 in the next eight years.

Idea 90: Quality circles

The achievement of excellence can only occur if the organization promotes a culture of creative dissatisfaction.

Unattributed

A quality circle is a group of 4 to 12 people from the same work area, performing similar work, who voluntarily meet on a regular basis to identify, investigate, analyze and solve their own work-related problems. The circle presents solutions to management and is usually involved in implementing and later monitoring them. Unlike suggestion schemes (see Idea 89), quality circles employ the principle of team creativity.

Quality circles were developed after the Second World War in Japan. It is traditionally important in Japan to 'gather the wisdom of the people'. Japanese industry, once so notorious for shoddy workmanship and low-quality merchandise, was transformed by accepting the gospel of quality. At one time it was estimated that 11 million Japanese were organized into quality circles, and children were taught in school the problem-solving techniques that these circles use.

Idea 91: Success factors for quality circles

Experience has shown that the following factors are very important for the success of quality circles:

◆ *Top leadership support* – the most senior leader in the division, company or department has to be seen to be committed to the programme, making it clear by word and example that he or she expects all the management team to give their active support. That means committing employee time for regular circle meetings, attending circle meetings when invited and helping approved solutions to be implemented.

◆ *Voluntary participation* – members and leaders of the circle are volunteers. Getting anything off the ground is much easier if people are not compelled to take part.

◆ *Training* – facilitators, leaders and members are properly trained in teamwork, in problem solving and in presentation skills. At the beginning of a programme, at least the facilitator (and often the first leaders) will have been trained by a consultant or other professionally competent resource. The facilitators often subsequently train leaders and help them in turn to train their circle members.

◆ *Shared work background* – the first circles will have been formed by people from the same work area. This shared work knowledge helps in faster development of the essential teamwork and also helps the circle members to contain problems to those under their direct control. In manufacturing, circles are usually formed from people doing similar work, but in service areas the members may be engaged in different aspects of a common process, such as dealing with orders or paying invoices.

◆ *Solution oriented* – circles work in a systematic way on solving problems (not just discussing them), investigating causes, looking for improvements, testing solutions and whenever possible being actively involved in implementation. The management must take care to see that suggested solutions are implemented once they have been accepted.

◆ *Recognition* – circles are not paid directly for their solutions, but management should arrange for proper recognition, for example by means of visits to special events or by contributions to social functions.

The main reason quality circles fail, it must be emphasized, is a lack of management support. They get off to a good start but rarely continue beyond the honeymoon period unless they are supported.

It follows that certain criteria should be present in an organization before quality circles can be successfully introduced. The company culture should be an open one, which encourages participation. There must also be a willingness to provide the relevant facts and information to enable employees to make an informed contribution. Industrial relations must be reasonably healthy. There should be a long-term commitment on the part of management at all levels, together with a readiness to provide the necessary training resources.

'The more you put into quality circles, the more you will get out of them.'

Idea 92: Checklist for testing the level of innovation within your organization

Innovation is our motto. The only trouble is that we do not practise it.

A middle manager

These 20 questions will give you a rating on where your organization stands in terms of innovation:

1 = poor   2 = average   3 = good   4 = very good
5 = excellent

- Rate your top executive management team's commitment to innovation.   1   2   3   4   5

- How far does the organization's vision emphasize the need for innovation?   1   2   3   4   5

- How well is that vision or philosophy communicated to all?   1   2   3   4   5

- Is your chief executive an enthusiastic leader of change?   1   2   3   4   5

- What is the level of mutual stimulation, feedback and constructive criticism?   1   2   3   4   5

- Assess the organization in terms of its internal teamwork.   1   2   3   4   5

- Is regular and effective use made of project teams?   1   2   3   4   5

- Are failures and errors accepted as part of the psychological contract in exchange for proper risk-taking?   1   2   3   4   5

- What is your record for retaining creative and talented young people?   1   2   3   4   5

- Are rewards, promotion or advancement linked at least in part to innovation?   1   2   3   4   5

◆ Evaluate the state of lateral communications.	1	2	3	4	5
◆ Are there plenty of informal opportunities for exchanging ideas?	1	2	3	4	5
◆ Rate your organization's freedom from 'if only' excuses.	1	2	3	4	5
◆ Are resources made available to support new initiatives?	1	2	3	4	5
◆ Assess the structural flexibility in the organization as a whole.	1	2	3	4	5
◆ Are decisions really pushed down to the lowest point at which they can be taken?	1	2	3	4	5
◆ Does everyone in the organization see themselves as involved in the innovative process?	1	2	3	4	5
◆ Has the organization adopted a long-term perspective over innovation?	1	2	3	4	5
◆ Is innovation part of an overall strategy for creating tomorrow's organization out of today's?	1	2	3	4	5
◆ Is it much fun to work in your organization?	1	2	3	4	5

Totals

How to interpret your score

70–100 Congratulations – you work in a highly innovative organization with a bright future.

40–69 Show some moral courage. Photocopy this checklist and take it to your chief executive as a means of raising the issue for urgent discussions. Remember also to take with you some positive suggestions.

10–39 Drastic action is needed if this organization wants to stay in business. In the meantime, get your parachute on.

Idea 93: The importance of training

Learning in old age is written in sand, but learning in youth is engraved on stone.

Arab proverb

Visualize the innovative organization as a *community of creativity*. From the directors downwards, every group in the organization sees itself as a team that is part of a yet wider team.

Creative interaction in groups and task teams for innovation will stimulate individual ideas. Individual thought or reflection will in turn feed back into group meetings or into the ongoing conversation of the organization as a whole.

No farmer, however, harvests the soil unless he or she invests in it. To operate an innovative organization with a culture of team creativity does presuppose a trained and educated workforce.

Apart from technical training, everyone today needs training in the skills and techniques of effective thinking: analyzing, synthesizing and valuing, and how the mind works – especially the positive part played by the unconscious mind in restructuring problems and providing solutions.

The foundations for such applied or practical thinking should be laid down firmly at school and university, but they need to be topped up and refuelled in the context of your own working environment.

A broader education is also to be encouraged, for an innovative organization is by definition also a learning organization. Anything that stirs up, excites or trains the 10,000 million brain cells of each team member is worth supporting.

> *'There are no national frontiers to learning.'*

Seven Greatest Ideas for Leading and Managing Innovation

Idea 94: Making your organization good at innovation

The business organization itself has to provide an environment in which creativity and innovation can flourish. The five hallmarks of those organizations that actually are good at innovation (not just paying lip service to it) are:

1 Top-level commitment.
2 Flexibility in organizational structure.
3 Tolerance of failure (and not risk aversion).
4 Encouragement of teamwork and innovation.
5 Skill in open and constructive communication.

Peter Drucker has said: 'Managing innovation . . . [is a] challenge to management . . . especially top management, and a touchstone of its competence.'

Organizations need to work at the main ingredients for success at managing innovation and apply themselves to the five hallmarks listed above.

1 Top-level commitment

This commitment must be visible and audible. Top management must ensure that blocks are removed and that inhibiting bureaucracy and individuals do not foul up the process. Chief executives and senior managers must value new ideas and innovation and participate actively to ensure that everyone knows of their commitment to positive and useful change. Sometimes the need for short-term profits can dull the edge of creativity and innovation. Only top management can prevent this happening – taking the long- not the short-term view.

2 *Flexibility in organizational structure*

The antithesis of the innovative organization is the bureaucratic one. Weber's characteristics of bureaucratic organizations are as follows:

- ◆ Impersonal and formal authority.
- ◆ Strong emphasis on functional specialization.
- ◆ A rule for every eventuality.
- ◆ Strong emphasis on hierarchy and status.
- ◆ Clearly laid down procedures (red tape).
- ◆ Proliferation of paperwork.
- ◆ Security of employment and advancement by seniority.

At the opposite end of the scale would be the flexible organization, which is one:

- ◆ Capable of responding to changing situations.
- ◆ Where barriers between staff in different areas are minimized.
- ◆ With a flat rather than pyramid-like organizational structure.
- ◆ Where decision-making is pushed downwards to where the organization meets its customers/suppliers.
- ◆ With entrepreneurial flair present at all levels.
- ◆ Which can develop and test more than one solution to problems encountered.
- ◆ With efficient rather than stifling monitoring systems.
- ◆ Which has enough discipline to get things done.
- ◆ Which balances freedom and order.

3 *Tolerance of failure*

Innovation and risk go hand in hand. Management that goes into critical overdrive when mistakes occur (rather than analyzing them to learn from the failures) smothers creativity and innovation. Risks can yield failure, but not taking risks can spell total disaster and an end to profits and growth.

Unless failure results from negligence, recklessness or complete incompetence, managers should not seek out scapegoats or exact revenge. Profits are the reward for taking risks and innovative organizations learn to live with risk.

4 Encouragement of teamwork and innovation

In innovation it can be said that none of us is as good as all of us. Teamwork and innovation are better in organizations where:

- ◆ The climate is open.
- ◆ Participation is encouraged.
- ◆ Facts and information are readily available.
- ◆ Change is managed positively.
- ◆ Resources are provided for training and development.
- ◆ Rules are at a minimum (with policies and guidelines instead).
- ◆ Internal communications are good and more by mouth than by memo.
- ◆ Respect is given to all colleagues (but not on demand by management – it has to be earned).
- ◆ Managers are themselves highly motivated.
- ◆ Teamwork often transcends departmental boundaries.

5 Skill at open and constructive communication

Communication should be good laterally and vertically; and flatter organizations should – in theory, at least – encourage good lateral communication. Managers should ensure a good flow of information so that ideas can emerge as a result. Cross-fertilization can create more (and better) ideas, particularly where departmental and divisional boundaries are crossed.

> *'None of us is as good as all of us, so build a community of creativity and innovation.'*

Idea 95: Plough up the ground

There is a natural opposition among men to anything they have not thought of themselves.

Sir Barnes Wallis, English engineer and inventor

No farmer sows seeds into hard, frozen or unyielding ground. You have to prepare the way for change. Unless you can create some creative dissatisfaction with things as they are, you cannot foster a willingness to change. Complacency is a greater enemy to change than fear. Indeed, complacency, arrogance and complexity are the three mortal diseases that bring great institutions down into the dust.

Like the prophets of old, go out into the highways and byways of your organization and cry out in a loud voice:

- ◆ A thing is not right because we do it.
- ◆ A method is not good because we use it.
- ◆ Equipment is not the best because we own it.

Your first target must be the assumptions and fixed ideas of your organization, the luggage it brings from its successful past. It is today's success that often breeds tomorrow's failure.

'It is not only what we have inherited from our fathers that exists again in us,' wrote Norwegian playwright Henrik Ibsen, 'but all sorts of old dead ideas and all kinds of old dead beliefs . . . They are not actually alive in us; but they are dormant, all the same, and we can never be rid of them.' Watch out for these skeletons in the cupboard.

Notice that innovation often comes when a fresh mind, untrammelled by dead ideas and assumptions, enters a traditional industry. Sir Henry Bessemer, the British civil engineer who invented the

Bessemer Process for converting molten pig-iron into steel, once said:

> *I had an immense advantage over many others dealing with the problem in as much as I had no fixed ideas derived from long-established practice to control and bias my mind, and did not suffer from the general belief that whatever is, is right.*

But in his case, as with many 'outsiders', ignorance and freedom from established patterns of thought in one field were joined with knowledge and training in other fields.

How do you plough up the ground? Ask plenty of questions, such as:

- ◆ Why are we doing it this way rather than any other?
- ◆ What are the criteria for success?
- ◆ What is the evidence that we are being successful?
- ◆ When did we last review these procedures?
- ◆ Who among our competitors is doing things differently and with what results?
- ◆ Where is the key research and development being done in this area?

'When a road is once built,' wrote Robert Louis Stevenson, 'it is a strange thing how it collects traffic, how every year as it goes on, more and more people are found to walk thereon, and others are raised up to repair and perpetuate it, and keep it alive.'

The kinds of questions listed above, repeated often, are like the points of a pneumatic drill digging up the hardened roads of organizational procedures. You cannot sow the seeds of desirable change on tarmac roads.

Idea 96: Market your ideas

The burden of proof is on you and your colleagues to persuade others in the organization, not least the top management, that the change you propose is a good one, namely a significant and cost-effective improvement on present practice.

As money is the language of business, you have to be able to show that at least in the middle term, the new idea or innovation will cut costs, add to profits or serve some other legitimate corporate interest. You sell ideas best by pointing out the benefits it will confer on the 'buyer', be he or she an external customer or an internal member of the same organization.

In the legal sphere it is a principle that no one should be allowed to act as judge in their own case. The same principle applies in innovation. Your own ideas do need to be subjected to critical evaluation by others.

'New ideas can be good or bad, just the same as old ones,' remarked US President Franklin D Roosevelt. Organizations, like society at large, have to protect themselves against needless innovation, including perhaps some of your less than brilliant brainwaves. The 'newer is truer' assumption is so often found to be a false one.

In a truly innovative organization, with developed team creativity at all levels, your critics will fortunately have open and positive minds. They will perceive the positive element in what you are proposing. They will test your ideas and, if necessary, reject them with tact. Or they may accept them and build on them, so that the process of innovation gets underway. You can help individuals and groups to see the value of a proposed change if you present it to them with skill.

Some creative thinkers are quite adept at finding their way through the political undergrowth of the organization. Others are not so good at presenting their ideas, getting them accepted and securing the necessary resources. That is where introducing a system of *project sponsors* can be such a help. Someone high in the organization is appointed to help the innovator gain access to resources and to protect the project when it falters.

Acting as a sponsor for an untried project is no picnic. Most sponsors, I believe, tend to bet on people rather than on products. As the proverb says, 'Captains bite their tongues until they bleed.' This means they have to keep their hands off the project. The first virtue of a sponsor is faith. The second is patience. And the third is understanding the differences between temporary setback and terminal problem.

It is at the level of the sponsor that there is a real opportunity to grow the seeds of innovation. Make sponsoring an explicit part of the job description for every top manager. When managers come in for appraisals, they should be asked about the new projects under their wing. The economics of projects is not the most important issue to raise. Always consider first the vision of the payoff.

In organizations that rate low in creativity and innovation, and do not appoint sponsors to act as godparents to new ideas, the process is considerably less effective and much more painful for all concerned.

American psychologist William James summed up a familiar pattern:

> *First a new theory is attacked as absurd; then it is admitted to be true but obvious and insignificant; finally it is seen to be so important that its adversaries claim that they themselves discovered it.*

In what ways can I improve my ability to market new ideas, both within the organization I work for and to potential customers?

Idea 97: Have a practice run

What is conservatism? Is it not adherence to the old and tried against the new and untried?

Abraham Lincoln, US President

Men and women tend not to believe in new things until they have had experience of them. Therefore why not suggest an experiment? If something is tried and tested, so that it can be matched against the present state, then it is much more likely to be accepted.

Remember that an *experiment* involves only a *limited commitment*. People are usually much more comfortable with that. It is only worth conducting, however, if there will be a fair and comprehensive review of the results. That does not preclude hard debate, for results are often open to several interpretations and it is important to arrive at the truth of the matter.

In the politics of innovation a proposal of a trial run – in, for example, one sector of the organization – is often an acceptable compromise as far as 'conservatives' are concerned. Its drawback is the extra time it adds to the bill. Indeed, it can be used merely as a delaying tactic by those who have no intention or willingness to change.

But it is always wise to assume the best motives in your adversaries and attribute to them the same rationality that you believe you possess yourself. In this way, they will surprise you by their willingness to change.

'Progress is the mother of problems,' wrote English writer G K Chesterton. You only have to contemplate the problems posed to us by the advance of science to see the truth of his statement. If any change is made there will be both *manifest* and *latent* consequences. The manifest consequences are the ones that can be foreseen; the latent ones only emerge during or after the innovation has been implemented.

Sometimes hindsight shows that the innovation has not yielded the promised benefits. Perhaps the original product or service had some quality that has been lost in the improvement? In that case, if it is not too late, why not revert to the original?

Hence the wisdom, if time permits, of conducting trials or experiments before adopting any innovation wholesale. Who wants to fly in a new aircraft that has not undergone rigorous test flights?

> *'Time spent on reconnaissance is seldom wasted.'*

Idea 98: Make change incremental

Organizational inertia is not entirely detrimental. Sometimes it protects individuals and groups within an organization from constant knee-jerk reactions to fluctuations in conditions, often engineered by mindless mercenary managers who are here today and gone tomorrow.

Only when change – social, economic and technological – is rapid in the environment does torpid inertia become a real liability. Rapid change calls for a rapid response.

Organizations that put their head in the sand and ignore change may find that they have to make sudden and relatively great changes in order to catch up and survive. This form of crisis management should be avoided. It arouses too much anxiety and fear about the personal consequences of change.

Gradual or incremental change is much better. As we have seen, innovation should always be evolutionary rather than revolutionary. Wearing these clothes it is much less threatening.

Therefore innovation should be planned in gradual stages, as part of a continuous process of adaptation to changing circumstances. It should not be a panic response to change that is now taking an organization by the throat because yesterday that same organization failed to take it by the hand.

Use the time available to communicate carefully about the need for change, experiment and review. 'Desire to have things done quickly prevents their being done thoroughly,' reflected Chinese philosopher Confucius. With innovation it is usually best to make haste slowly.

'An inch is a cinch, a yard is hard.'

Idea 99: Communicate about innovation

Good communication supplies a vital dimension in the climate that fosters innovation. You as an individual manager have your share in the responsibility for ensuring that it happens. That means that you should:

◆ Seize opportunities to talk to your people about the importance of new ideas for improving the product range and reducing costs. Give examples and tell stories of changes that have been successfully implemented.

◆ Explain why suggested ideas have been accepted or rejected for further investigation and development. What are the selection criteria for ideas? Give your team regular progress updates on the passage through the organization of ideas that originated with its discussions.

◆ Give recognition and reward appropriately. The most powerful communication of all comes from the ideas that really do make a difference for the better to your business.

Remember that progress motivates. If you never give people feedback they will soon lose interest. Remember, too, that change – innovative change – may be exciting to you, a vista of new opportunity. But to others in your organization it may appear to be a threat. Does it, for example, involve job losses? Or reduction in take-home pay? Or more unsocial hours of work?

Make sure that you bear in mind the individual needs circle (see Idea 65) when you communicate about necessary and desirable corporate change. If you can demonstrate that the innovation, be it large or small, benefits the individuals who will have to implement it, as well as the common good, your task of improvement becomes a lot easier. So be truthful – and be prepared to spend a lot of time talking!

'The willing bird flies further than the thrown stone.'

Idea 100: Leadership is essential

Not the cry but the flight of the wild duck leads the flock to fly and follow.

Chinese proverb

The principal obstacles to innovative change and improvement are seldom technical or financial – they are human. It takes real leadership at all levels – team, operational and strategic – to transform a conservative organization into an innovative one. But that is what you are being paid to do.

If you happen to be a strategic leader, that is doubly true. For one certain fact about innovation is that if the top leadership is not committed to and enthusiastic about change, it will not happen.

Why? Because there is an element of risk in even the best prepared and planned innovation. Not all the consequences or side-effects can be foretold. There is plenty of room for uncertainty and fear.

Leaders of innovation need to show moral courage, commitment and enthusiasm if they are to keep people moving on the path of progress. They should learn to share their courage and conceal their fear.

Again and again, ask yourself: Do I have an alternative? There are too many challenges and problems outside the organization awaiting attention without you having continually to expend too much time and energy overcoming negative resistance to change within it.

Our journey together in this book has come to an end. For my part I have greatly enjoyed it, and I trust that you have as well. You are welcome to steal some or all of these 100 Great Ideas and make them your own. The only price is that you must be willing to use them.

I hope, too, that your journey as a creative leader and manager will continue. If I may borrow the words of a seventeenth-century German poet, Angelus Silesius:

> *Friend, you have read enough.*
> *If you desire still more,*
> *then be the odyssey yourself,*
> *and all that it stands for.*

Follow-up test

Building innovative organizations

- ☐ Have you experienced failures to innovate in time because of lack of commitment on the part of top management?
- ☐ 'I have never met a man so ignorant,' said Italian astronomer Galileo, 'that I couldn't learn something from him.' Can you list five ideas for improving products or services that you have learned from the people who are doing the work today?
- ☐ How many feasible and actionable ideas for improvement did your company's suggestion scheme net in the last calendar year?
- ☐ Do you have a fit-for-purpose system of quality circles in your organization?
- ☐ Does your organization provide training opportunities in creativity and innovation?

Leading and managing innovation

- ☐ Do your colleagues as leaders and managers accept their responsibility for sustained innovation?
- ☐ 'You cannot expect a harvest of useful ideas if you don't plough up the ground.' What have you done in the last six months to make your organization more fertile?
- ☐ Have you experienced failures because you did not market your ideas effectively? What lessons did you learn?

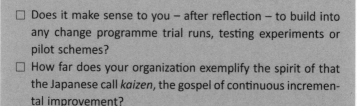

☐ Does it make sense to you – after reflection – to build into any change programme trial runs, testing experiments or pilot schemes?

☐ How far does your organization exemplify the spirit of that the Japanese call *kaizen*, the gospel of continuous incremental improvement?

☐ Can anyone, in your opinion, really aspire to be a leader if they have no ideas and no concern at all for innovation?

☐ How do you plan to continue your own journey of learning to be a more creative leader?

Appendix

The nine dots (Idea 7)

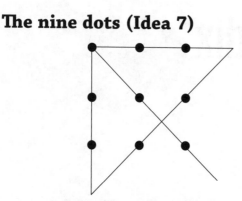

The reason you may not have been able to solve the problem is that unconsciously your mind imposed a framework around the nine dots. You have to go beyond that invisible box. From this problem, which I introduced in 1969, comes the phrase 'Think outside the box!'

The six matchsticks

Again, ask yourself the reason you couldn't solve it. Were you making an assumption or imposing a constraint that the puzzle must be solved on one plane or in two dimensions?

Breaking out of the two-dimensional unconscious assumption and into three dimensions gives the most elegant solution:

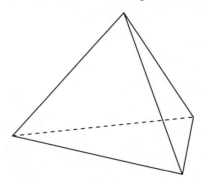

The six coins

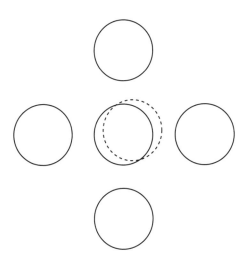

Move the bottom coin up and place it on bottom of the centre coin. Now the coins add up to four, both horizontally and vertically.

Again, it is an unconscious assumption – that the coins cannot be placed on top of each other – that may have prevented you from solving the problem.

Solutions to analogy exercises (Idea 50)

Exercise 1

a   A young English designer named Carwardine approached the firm of Herbert Terry at the beginning of the 1930s with the proposal that they should build a desk light employing the constant-tension jointing principles found in the human arm. The company agreed, and the

Anglepoise light was the result. From that time it has been in production, scarcely altered except for details and finishes.

b   Cat's eyes in the road.

c   Spitfires.

d   Clarence Birdseye took a vacation in Canada and saw some salmon that had been naturally frozen in ice and then thawed. When they were cooked he noticed how fresh they tasted. He borrowed the idea and the mighty frozen food industry was born.

e   They could have suggested the principle of independent suspension.

f   The burrowing movement of earthworms has suggested a new method of mining, which is now in commercial production.

g   In the Edinburgh Royal Botanic Gardens there is a plaque commemorating a flower that inspired the design of the Crystal Palace.

h   Sir Basil Spence, the architect of Coventry Cathedral, was flipping through the pages of a natural history magazine when he came across an enlargement of the eye of a fly, and that gave him the general lines for the vault.

i   Linear motors.

j   Ball-and-socket joints.

Exercise 3

a   Magnifying glasses.

b   The arch. Possibly the Eskimos were the first to use the arch in the construction of igloos.

c   Hollow steel cylinders.

d   Levers.

e   Bagpipes.

f   Wind instruments.

Solution to invention/occupation exercise (Idea 54)

Invention	*Inventor's main occupation*
Ballpoint pen	Sculptor
Safety razor	Traveller in corks
Kodachrome films	Musician
Automatic telephone	Undertaker
Parking meter	Journalist
Pneumatic tyre	Veterinary surgeon
Long-playing record	Television engineer

Answer to the secret of Japanese success (Idea 88)

'You won't do it.'

Answer to suggestion scheme exercise (Idea 89)

The man contributed more than 20,000 suggestions over 40 years.

About John Adair

John Adair is the business guru who invented Action Centred Leadership (ACL) in the 1970s, now one of the best-known leadership models in the world. Organizations worldwide use it to develop their leadership capability and management skills. ACL is being successfully applied in engineering companies, retailers, local authorities, financial institutions and universities. The British armed services base their leadership training on it.

John's company, Adair International, provides ACL development programmes, Accredited Trainer programmes and consultancy around the world, via regional partnerships with training providers in the UK, Australia, New Zealand, the Middle East and India.

John is the author of more than 40 books, translated into many languages, and numerous articles on history, leadership and management development.

Index

ALSO AVAILABLE...

9780857081155   9780857081148   9780857081308

9780857081315   9780857081018   9780857081506   9780857082046

...and there's more to come!

CAPSTONE
be inspired!